D1444847

DISCOURSE OF REASON

DISCOURSE
OF REASON

A Brief Handbook of Semantics and Logic

SECOND EDITION

JOHN C. SHERWOOD
University of Oregon

HARPER & ROW, PUBLISHERS
New York, Evanston, and London

LIBRARY OF CONGRESS CATALOG CARD NUMBER: 64–12792

CONTENTS

v

CONTENTS

PREFACE

The intent of *Discourse of Reason* remains what it was in the first edition: to present such portions of logic and semantics as an English teacher might profitably expound to his composition classes as a help to them in solving the practical problems of communication. The text has been revised throughout in line with my own second thoughts and the suggestions of friends; some illustrative material has been added, especially in Chapter V. Because many teachers find them useful, an explanation of the Venn diagram and a list of common fallacies have been supplied as appendixes.

JOHN C. SHERWOOD

DISCOURSE OF REASON

I

SEMANTICS: *Denotation*

I

SEMANTICS: Denotation

The supreme importance of language in human affairs is not likely to be underestimated by any literate human being; if anything, this importance has been somewhat exaggerated in our time, so that it is a kind of fad to attribute all sorts of social and intellectual ills to the misuse of words. Our concern with language is obvious from the number of academic disciplines that deal with it. Grammar, rhetoric, linguistics, semantics—all are areas of active investigation. They are not always sharply distinct from each other, but they have separate traditions and will probably remain somewhat apart because they represent different forms of interest and have different practical uses. In no sense, of course, need they be in conflict; rather, they should (as in fact they do) supplement each other. Each is a valid discipline that anyone concerned with the use of language should explore.

A convenient scheme for classifying the problems of language is one which distinguishes in terms of the relationships which words by their nature possess. A given word may be regarded as having three relationships: (1) a relationship with the other words with which it is used, (2) a relationship with the persons who utter and hear it, and (3) a relationship with the thing it represents (the *referent*). The relationships of words with each other are a matter of grammar, for grammar is not primarily a set of prohibitions (though it may be so taught) but a set of rules for combining the different classes of words into intelligible sequences. The relationship of a word to the thing or things it represents is the primary and proper area of concern for academic semantics, but some semanticists have also concerned themselves very usefully with the relationships between words and people. Here semantics tends to overlap rhetoric, but with this significant difference: rhetoric is traditionally an art of persuasion, a set of devices to enable us to move the emotions of others with words, whereas this type of semantics has been concerned partly with studying the emotional effects of language theoretically, and partly with helping us to understand the emotional effects of words in order to resist those effects when others attempt to employ them on us—a purpose almost opposite to the aims of rhetoric. Understandably, the more philosophical semanticists have tended to be concerned with the first aspect, and the more popular writers with the second.

For our present purposes it is enough to notice that the meaning of most words has two overlapping yet distinguishable aspects. A word has its *denotation,* a certain set of things in the world which it stands for and points to; but it also has its *connotation,* a set of feelings and associations which it arouses in the people who use it. The word "traitor" denotes the kind of person who has "given aid and comfort to the enemy in time of war," but it has in addition all sorts of unpleasant associations based on our natural attitudes toward traitors. The discussion of semantics included here is built around these two aspects. Denotation is the subject of the present chapter, connotation of the chapter that follows.

Words as Symbols

At first glance it might seem that a study of denotation would be superfluous and that no educated user of language could ever forget that words stand for things: how otherwise could they be of use to us? Still it is well to remind ourselves, first, that words are signs, objects whose real value lies in the fact that they *point* to something else; and, second, that they are the particular kind of sign called a *symbol*. Symbols differ from certain other types of signs in that the connection between the sign and the thing it points to is entirely a matter of human convention. A cloud is a sign of rain because it brings the rain, and a weathervane is a sign of the wind because the wind controls it, but there is no special reason why a tool used for digging should have the sign "spade," except that speakers of English, through long usage and custom, have chosen to make it so. Verbal symbolism is even more arbitrary than some other kinds of symbolism. A cross naturally suggests Christianity, just as a sword suggests war, or a skull death, but there is no natural reason why we should say "dog" when the Frenchman says "chien." Words, then, are symbols of things—but two qualifications are in order. Certain types of words are perhaps not strictly symbolic or are symbolic only in a very special way; such are prepositions and conjunctions, whose real function is syntactical, the function of joining other words together.[1] Furthermore, the things

[1] It is simplest to discuss the symbolism of words in terms of nouns, which often have very tangible referents to point to, but verbs, adjectives, and adverbs have their referents in classes of actions, qualities, and the like.

symbolized—the referents—are of the most various kinds.

Words may stand for existing objects such as bathing suits and unabridged dictionaries; for possible or imagined objects, such as Martians and unicorns; for qualities, both physical and moral, such as hardness and goodness; for thoughts and feelings, states, actions, and events, classes and groups, abstractions, concepts, and relations. Often the thing represented is quite complex, or may have existence only in our own minds. What is the "thing" to which the name "England" corresponds—a plot of ground, a people, a government, a culture, or the sum of all? And if we feel that we can easily define England in terms of measured boundaries, what about such a term as "Western Civilization," whose chronological and geographical limits we could never define with any exactitude? What, too, are the things to which the poet's "imagination" and the psychoanalyst's "id" correspond? Can we point to the section of the brain that contains them? Now all these terms are useful and even necessary, and we should not hold them suspect because we cannot feel or handle their referents. We must keep in mind, however, that behind words lie not merely tangible objects, but a miscellaneous collection of physical and mental phenomena of differing degrees and kinds of material reality, and that the existence of a word is no assurance of the existence of a corresponding object outside the mind.

It is equally important to remember that no mystic bond connects the word to its referent. A few words only seem to have a natural appropriateness, chiefly onomatopoeic words like "hiss" and "murmur." Yet not only the ordinary people who shout at foreigners to make them understand but great thinkers often speak as if each thing had one word which belonged to it by right and to no other. Plato argues that the letters composing a word are (or ought to be) an indication of the thing represented; while Bacon, in order to arrive at the nature of heat, analyzes all the objects to which men have applied the term "hot," from fire to pepper, and Aristotle believes that, even when a word has several senses, there is something common to them all. Actually the relationship is a rather shifty and unstable business. One word may serve to designate a series of quite unrelated objects; a railroad train is something very different from the train of a wedding gown, though the idea of towing or pulling is present in both. Words also shift their meanings in the process of time. "Marshal" once meant a farrier, but now designates the highest kind of military officer; "prove" once meant "test" and now usually means "establish." A "knight" is a nobleman, but the German cognate "Knecht" now means a servant. A guinea pig is not a pig and does not come from Guinea. Any lingering illusion about a natural correspondence between words and things should disappear if we have occasion to translate from one language to another. Sometimes there are words in one language for which the other has no equivalent; we cannot express our idea of "home" with any single French word, while for the expressive French "patrie" we can only offer the clumsy German-sounding "fatherland." Foreign words for colors may not even correspond to ours; Whatmough reports that Welsh, Navaho, and Latin do not distinguish green from blue, and to Homer the sea is the color of wine. Mark Twain laments comically that the German "Zug" and "Schlag" can mean anything, but what would a German say of our "get" and "case"? Beginning students may attempt word-for-word translations, but scholars know better.

In the seventeenth century certain thinkers dreamed of

a language in which the correspondence of words and things would be stable and reliable; Swift makes fun of them in his picture of a group of scientists who have lost all faith in words and communicate by pointing at objects. The dream, we know now, is futile. The world around us does not consist of a definite number of easily distinguishable objects to be named as Adam named the animals. It is, as William James called it, a "booming, buzzing confusion" out of which we select a certain number of phenomena considered worthy enough for the assignment of words. Whether a thing will have a name or not depends on our feelings and interests and the framework of our thinking. A vocabulary that covered the whole of existence would be infinitely large or at least beyond the capacity of human memory; it would be as useless as a map made to the same scale as the area it represented. *Punch* imagines a Greek word meaning "chalk under the fingernails of sixth form masters," but this seems a trivial object to have a word to itself, and most of the time we are more selective. Because domestic animals have been so important to human economy, we frequently devise, for a given animal, not merely a name for the species, but names for different sexes, ages, and types—horse, stallion, mare, gelding, colt, Percheron. In naming dinosaurs we are content with a name for the species; it seems unnecessary to have a special term for a baby female *tricerotops*. The existence of a word is usually attributable to our need for it.

Largely by necessity, then, words (other than proper nouns) stand not for individual objects but for classes of objects; hence to use a certain word is to indicate that the object which it denotes belongs to the same class as certain other objects, which by accepted usage are called by the same name. To speak of a "bat" is to say that the object of discussion is a mammal that can fly and has certain other known characteristics; if we are careful, that is all we understand it to mean. Some words classify in terms of more characteristics than others. To call a creature a "dog" is to say more about it than to call it a "mammal"; the latter word designates a very large class of beings with relatively few qualities in common.

By the nature of things words classify, and by the nature of things they also abstract. When we call an animal a "dog" we do so because it has certain biological characteristics—four legs, warm blood, certain kinds of teeth, and so on; when we call it a "domestic animal" we mean that it is kept for use by human beings; when we call it "man's best friend" we are talking about its loyalty. In each case we abstract, that is, we isolate certain aspects of the denoted object, leaving others out of account. To call a man a "criminal" is to consider him solely with reference to his conduct on certain occasions, without reference to anything else in his character or situation.

The classifications which common words make, unlike the classes marked out by scientific terminology, are often very unsystematic and illogical. The words we use to designate ethnic groups other than our own show this lack of system: sometimes they classify in terms of geography or nationality (Swiss), sometimes by language (Bantu), sometimes by real or supposed physical characteristics (Indian). Classification varies in extent and in kind from language to language as well. In the language of the Cuna, a Central American Indian group, animals have different names by day and by night; in English we do not make such distinctions. Sometimes we decide to alter our classifications, and

a whale ceases to be a fish, though if we classified solely on
the basis of shape and habitat it would remain a fish. Sometimes we have difficulty deciding whether the word applies
or not: is a Neanderthal man or an unborn child a human
being? No one disputes the salient characteristics of a cave
man or an embryo, but we may not all agree that they are
properly denoted by the term "human being."

General, Vague, and Ambiguous Terms

Normally we answer the questions of *word choice* by ad-
vising a careful use of the dictionary, a respect for correct
usage, and the use of concrete terms. (A semanticist would
add: Keep your eye on the referent!) Teachers tend to em-
phasize these points and with good reason, since the beginning writer often tends to be careless and vague; but
emphasizing these points alone oversimplifies the matter.
Words may be general, they may be vague, or they may be
ambiguous. A word is general if it designates a very large
number of objects with little in common: words like "animal," "vehicle," or "tool." A word is vague if the boundaries of its denotation are indistinct: we could hardly hope
to frame an ironclad distinction between "hill" and "moun-
tain," or between "large" and "small." A small elephant is
larger than a large ant, and our idea of a small car has
changed a good deal in the last few years. A word is ambiguous if it has several accepted meanings: we must decide
from the context whether "table" means a piece of furni-
ture or a column of figures. The word "plant" is general
because it refers to half the living creation, the word "similar" is vague because we are not sure of the degree and
kind of resemblance intended between compared things,
and the word "ash" is ambiguous because it might refer to
a tree or the residue of a fire. It would be easy to suggest

that we avoid such words but hard to do so in practice. We would hardly wish to avoid general terms anyway; they are the means by which we indicate broad relations and large classes. We need the general term "institution" to cover in a broad way the social units which we describe more specifically as colleges, prisons, asylums, and so on; they have something in common which the name serves to suggest. Vague words too have their uses; we can never define absolutely the words "some" or "several," but we need such words all the same. In general, we say, we should be as definite and concrete as is possible and appropriate. Merely as a matter of vividness we may prefer the particular to the general, but the specific term is not necessarily more exact and may even be less clear than the inclusive general term. We can sometimes escape from vagueness by statistics and speak of a six-footer instead of a tall man, but too much precision would be pedantic. Often a vague word becomes specific in context; we could not say how tall "tall" is, but we could say within a few inches how tall a tall man is. Context tends to take care of ambiguous words also. The term "buffalo" is somewhat ambiguous, since our early settlers applied the term (which in the old world designates what we call a "water buffalo") to an animal equivalent to the European bison, and in a scientific or legal context we should have to be pedantic and call it a "bison"; but in such specific sentences as "The Sioux hunted the buffalo" there is no ambiguity. Moderate care and exactness, varying with the occasion, is what is needed, not a deep suspiciousness of all but the most concrete terms.

Words as Labels

The failure to understand the symbolic nature of language and to distinguish clearly between words and the things they stand for can have serious practical consequences. To be able to call something by its right name is satisfying, for it makes us feel that we understand the situation. The feeling of satisfaction may not always be justified. We are ill and experience a series of well-defined symptoms; the doctor comes and gives a name to them: pneumonia, endocarditis, neurasthenia, and we feel comforted by knowing the name of what is annoying us. Perhaps the comfort is justified, because the doctor's use of the term means that he understands the nature of the disorder and the proper method of treatment; but perhaps the name is a mere *label* for the symptoms, and we know no more than we did before. (Sometimes too a term that is meaningful to the doctor is a mere label to the patient.) Early chemistry had a term "phlogiston," designating a substance supposed to be weightless, odorless, and intangible; it was thought to be the cause of fire. We know today, of course, that phlogiston has no existence at all; but the early chemist, equipped with his label, thought he had understood the cause of fire. In literary criticism and the social sciences we are in special danger of confusing labeling with analysis or investigation, and to throw about terms such as "urban," "unconscious," "irony," and "empathy," instead of looking at the thing itself. Such labeling is not entirely futile; it communicates something of the speaker's opinion, but not always much information.

Even when labeling is moderately informative, it may do us a disservice by stopping thought; having applied the label, we do not feel obliged to go further. The driver is a "woman," hence erratic; the professor is a "Red," hence dangerous; the girl is "Irish," hence black-haired, blue-eyed, charming, warm-hearted, and impulsive. There is a special danger when we use racial designations in that way. Terms like "wog" are hardly a *cause* of prejudice. Rather they serve to express the prejudices we already feel on the basis of economic or political rivalry or our primitive fears of the strange and unknown; yet even so they can do a great deal of damage by helping to confirm or continue prejudices we might otherwise outgrow and by infecting others with the same feelings. Even the ordinary, neutral names for races have to be used with care. A term such as "German" is, to begin with, ambiguous; it may refer to present or former citizenship, to language, to place of residence, or possibly to race, assuming that it is possible to identify a German race as distinct from inhabitants of Germany or people who speak German. To call a person "German" is to say one of these things and (if we are careful) to do no more. There is a German culture differing somewhat from ours, and we could probably make a fairly plausible list of ways in which the average German differs from the average American, but the differences among individuals are so great that we could never assume that the person we have labeled will have all the average characteristics of his class. *Life* magazine reports the case of a man who, once classified as "feeble-minded," remained imprisoned in an institution for fifty-nine years, though he could play eight musical instruments, was a skilled printer, and was gentle and amiable. If we can keep in mind that words classify and abstract, we may come closer to avoiding such errors.

These problems go beyond single words. It is possible to write whole passages and even books in which we do little more than manipulate labels. Many readers would doubt whether the following learned and ingenious passage (in a style of philosophizing now out of fashion) adds much to the sum of human knowledge:

> . . . It is urged that "thought implies a thinker," that thought without a thinker is inconceivable. This difficulty is only a recrudescence of the difficulty which the common mind experiences in understanding how anything can be real and yet not exist. What this assertion means is that thoughts cannot *exist* except in the mind of a thinker. And this is perfectly true. Every existence is an individual entity which is *there,* at some place or time. An existent thought must be such an individual entity, which is there, which is present at this particular time in the stream of some particular consciousness. But universals do not exist and are therefore not present in a stream of consciousness, in a mind. Thoughts cannot *exist* without a thinker. But universals do not *exist.* They are *real.*[2]

To some philosophers, obviously, these words would seem interesting and significant; but to the "common mind" to whom the author condescendingly alludes, the passage would seem a mere playing with words, a maneuvering with labels which has no clear reference to any objective reality. Not many writers today would start out at such a high level of abstraction; it is easier gradually to lose touch with concrete referents and ascend by stages into the clouds. *The Lonely Crowd,* a deservedly influential book, sometimes tends in this direction:

The era of economic abundance and incipient population decline calls for the work of men whose tool is symbolism and whose aim is some observable response from people. These manipulators, of course, are not necessarily other-directed in character. Many inner-directed people are successful manipulators of people; often, their very inner-direction makes them unaware of how much they do manipulate and exploit others.

[2] W. T. Stace, *The Philosophy of Hegel,* New York, 1955, pp. 28–29.

Nevertheless, for manipulating others, there is a somewhat greater compatibility between characterological other-direction and sensitivity to others' subtler wants.[3]

Generally Professor Riesman and his colleagues are careful to remember that "other-direction" (conformity to the standards of the group) and "inner-direction" (obedience to inner convictions) stand for very complex phenomena and are not in themselves explanations at all. An incautious reader, however, might easily drift into a position where the term "other-direction" became for him a convenient label and an impediment rather than a stimulus to thought.

Arguing About Words

Another pitfall in the use of words is the tendency to argue about terms when there is no real dispute about the facts of the case. William James illustrates the point with the following puzzle: A man is pursuing a squirrel around a tree. The squirrel circles, clinging to the bark, so that the trunk always conceals him from the man. Both man and squirrel are going around the tree; is the man going around the squirrel? Here there is no dispute about the movements of man or squirrel, but only about the relevance of the term "around": the argument is, in a practical sense at least, quite trivial. Such quibbling is common in literary criticism. John Dryden wonders whether *The Faerie Queene* is a genuine epic, Samuel Johnson doubts whether Shakespeare's plays are true tragedies, and some modern editors try to call the Book of Job a drama; in none of these cases is there a question of what the work is really like or even of its literary merit but only of the definition of a term. Necessarily verbal disputes sometimes acquire

3 David Riesman, *et al.*, *The Lonely Crowd*, New York, 1953, p. 153.

practical consequences, especially when the disputed words occur in a law or regulation. In Ellis Parker Butler's "Pigs Is Pigs," the express agent and his customer argue as to whether a shipment of guinea pigs should pay the rate for *pets* or the higher rate for *pigs*. The dispute can hardly be called pointless, since money is involved, though the agent is obviously more concerned with words than facts, or he would see that for all practical purposes the animals are pets. Disputes about important questions of fact or value may take the *form* of disputes about words; it is only the dispute in which nothing is at stake but the term which is idle and foolish.

A final error is the failure, accidental or deliberate, to keep to the same meaning of a term throughout a discussion. The hedonist argues that pleasure is the only motive for human action and that the philanthropist and the martyr give up their possessions and lives because sacrifice is what gives them pleasure. Before we give ourselves up to cynicism, however, let us notice that, although in the beginning of the argument "pleasure" seems to have its normal meaning of pleasant satisfactions, by the end of the argument it seems to mean simply whatever line of conduct we voluntarily choose. The argument is not only cynical but nearly meaningless or at best tautological, saying that we do what we wish to do because we wish to do it. A television program celebrated what passes in mass-communication circles for "faith." The theme was illustrated by three examples: a minister's faith that his bankrupt church would be able to stay open (an eccentric millionaire subsequently sent him a million dollars), his faith that a little boy run over by a truck had achieved immortality, and his faith that an untested pneumonia vaccine just invented by his prospective son-in-law would cure, not kill, his ailing daughter (needless to say, it cured her). The second variety of faith we recognize as normal Christian faith, but the "faith" in the vaccine is either a calculated risk based on a rational appraisal of the doctor's character and scientific stature, or it is no better than the faith that keeps cancer quacks in business. As for a faith that depends for its fulfillment on the generosity of eccentric millionaires, it has neither a rational nor a theological basis and is bound to be frequently disappointed.

Definition

One obvious escape from verbal disputes is the careful definition of terms. Definition often consists merely in offering a synonym, but since there are few exact synonyms in English, careful definition requires something more. A convenient formula, though open to certain logical objections (it really defines the thing rather than the word), is Aristotle's *genus* and *differentia*. We tell to what general class (*genus*) the referent of the word belongs and then enumerate the characteristics (*differentia*) which distinguish it from other members of the class. Consider, for instance, the following definitions from the *New English Dictionary;* the genus is in italics, the remainder of the definition constituting the differentia:

VESSEL: Any *structure* designed to float upon and traverse the water for the carriage of persons or goods.

SHIP: A large sea-going *vessel*.

WARSHIP: A *ship* armed and manned for war.

BATTLESHIP: A *warship* of the largest and most heavily armored class.

The "extended definition," in which a term is defined at length in a short essay, though a useful exercise, is rather a description than a definition, since it goes far beyond what is necessary to show the correct use of the word or to identify the referent.

The necessity for defining terms in controversy arises from the fact that so many words in English have more than one accepted meaning; the definition serves to inform the reader as to which of the possible meanings the writer intends to use. A discussion of the "teaching of English" can only lead to futility if the writer means by "English" the teaching of composition and the reader assumes that he is referring to the whole field of "English," including literature.

Not infrequently in controversy we encounter definitions which cannot honestly be regarded as corresponding to ordinary usage, but which are obviously manufactured especially to support the argument, as in the following instance:

Vivisection is experimenting with living beings, and that's just what "liberals" are doing today—carrying out experiments on living people to see if they can stand them. Progressive education, socialized medicine, stealing money from the taxpayer to support bureaucracy—it's all vivisection.

If "vivisection" were used in the ordinary sense, it would obviously not be applicable to progressive education or socialized medicine; the definition has been distorted in order to get a certain effect. Some philosophers have argued that propositions should be considered meaningless, except as expressions of feeling, unless they can be verified by reference to empirical facts. Thus such propositions as "God is love" would be regarded, under this definition, as purely emotive, without any intellectual content. Now it is clear that the definition of "meaning" here employed is a rather unusual one, not in accord with common usage; it is in fact not so much a definition in the dictionary sense as a statement of a rather dubious philosophical position. Given the right to define terms according to our own ca-price, we could prove any proposition, no matter how absurd.

Conclusions

Words, then, are symbols whose arbitrary relationships to the things they represent must always be kept in mind if we are to avoid the pitfalls that interfere with rational dis-course. Not only must we be very careful in using vague and general terms; we must scrupulously refrain from sub-stituting labeling for learning, from quarreling about terms, and from allowing shifts of meaning to unsettle our arguments.

Exercises in Denotation

EXERCISE A

Distinguish carefully the words in the following groups of synonyms or related words.

1. Love, affection, lust, kindness, friendship, attachment, mu-tual attraction, emotional involvement, fondness, liking, de-votion.
2. Goodness, virtue, righteousness, honesty, decency, honor, integrity, piety, rectitude, correctness (in conduct).
3. School, university, college, institution, institute.
4. Race, folk, people, population, inhabitants.

EXERCISE B

Upon what basis would a person be classified as belonging to each of the following ethnic groups? In other words, what characteristics would he need to have to belong to each?

Anglo-Saxon, Slav, Turk, Armenian, Ainu, Mexican, Mayan, Hawaiian, Eskimo, Macedonian, Greek, Latin-American, Pennsylvania Dutch, Yankee, Israeli, Hebrew, Arab, Berber, Moor, Tyrolese, Irish, Parsee, Samaritan, Abyssinian, Boer.

EXERCISE C

Is a corporation a person (legally)? Is a bazooka a cannon? Is a hut a house? Is a saber a sword? Is a jeep a truck? Is *Ulysses* a novel? Is a platypus a mammal? Is a reformatory a prison? Are finance charges interest? Do any of these questions have practical implications?

EXERCISE D

Comment on the use of terminology in the following passages, looking especially for shifts of meaning or deceptive deviations from common usage. Not all the examples are faulty.

1. Business is business. A penny saved is a penny earned.

2. No race is inferior; in fact, some are superior.

3. Removing controversial comic books from circulation is not censorship. It is simply planning for school children the right kind of reading.

4. "I don't feel like myself any more. . . . I just never feel like myself." (Character in "The Enormous Radio") "This isn't the real me you're seeing." (Thurber cartoon)

5. The United States must be a welfare state, since the Constitution charges the government with promoting the general welfare.

6. "Doubtless it is unnatural to be drunk. But then in a real sense it is unnatural to be human." (G. K. Chesterton)

7. Nude pictures are not to be condemned, for art is the representation of nature, and nature is the human body.

8. "A pickpocket is obviously a champion of private enterprise." (Chesterton)

9. Man can't repeal the law of gravity, nor can he repeal the law of supply and demand.

10. The company didn't really make a profit of nine cents

on the dollar last year; four cents of the nine had to be payed to the stockholders for the use of their money.

11. Increase in divorce rates does not indicate disruption of the family. It indicates greater freedom of choice and a more congenial type of marriage.

12. "By and large, of every 200 boys and girls who enter a senior high school from a junior high or an elementary school, 200 of them are normal. They become subnormals and above-normals in the thinking of teachers only if those teachers have rather fixed ideas of a ninth- or tenth-grade curriculum in English, history, or what not. . . . It is normal for some children to be noisier than others, for some to be more active, some to be poorer readers, some to be less tidy, some to be less co-operative, some to be more dictatorial, and so on." (*Some Principles of Teaching*)

Exercise E

Analyze and compare the definitions of freedom stated or implied in the following passages. What practical consequences follow from accepting one definition rather than another?

1. "The spokesmen for these special interests say that these programs [social security, etc.] make the Government too powerful and cause the people to lose their freedom. Well, now, that is just not so. Programs like these make people more independent—independent of the government, independent of big business and corporate power.

"People who have the opportunity to work and earn, and who have an assured income for old age, are free. They are free of public or private charity. They can live happier, more useful lives. That's real freedom." (Harry S Truman)

2. ". . . Freedom is often understood to mean somebody's freedom from interference to make a personal profit. Freedom can yet be understood to mean freedom to make a good society for all." (Robert Redfield)

3. "You hear every day greater numbers of foolish people speaking about liberty, as if it were such an honourable thing; so far from being that, it is, on the whole, and in the broadest

sense, dishonourable, and an attribute of the lower creatures. No human being, however great, or powerful, was ever so free as a fish. There is always something that he must, or must not do; while the fish may do whatever he likes. . . . The Sun has no liberty—a dead leaf has much." (John Ruskin)

4. "Liberty? The true liberty of a man, you would say, consisted in his finding out, or being forced to find out the right path, and to walk thereon. To learn, or to be taught, what work he actually was able for; and then by permission, persuasion, and even compulsion, to set about doing of the same! That is his true blessedness, honour, 'liberty' and maximum of wellbeing: if liberty be not that, I for one have small care about liberty. You do not allow a palpable madman to leap over precipices; you violate his liberty. . . . Every stupid, every cowardly and foolish man is but a less palpable madman: his true liberty were that a wiser man, that any and every wise man, could, by brass collars, or whatever milder or sharper way, lay hold of him when he was going wrong, and order and compel him to go a little righter." (Thomas Carlyle)

5. "A man is free, first, when he can eat, drink, dress, and live as and where he pleases or finds necessary; second, when he can wander out into the world whenever and however he pleases; and, third, when others honor and esteem his labors. That is the true meaning of freedom." (Dr. Robert Ley, Nazi official)

6. "The experiences of the Chinese people in these few decades instruct us to enforce a democratic dictatorship by people, or, in other words, the dictatorship of the people. It means the deprivation of the reactionaries of their right to voice. Only the people are entitled to speak. . . . The combination of the democracy for the people and the dictatorship over the reactionaries means democratic dictatorship by people." (Mao Tsetung)

7. ". . . In a very important sense, Americans today are not free men, free women. . . . We are slaves to a false theory of human life. We seek to build a nation on self-seeking, self-expression, self-assertion. . . . If 'sin' means 'selfishness,' and

it means just that, then we Americans are not free; we are *slaves to sin.*" (Bernard Iddings Bell)

8. "Freedom . . . is not what Sir Robert Filmer tells us: 'A liberty for every one to do what he lists, to live as he pleases, and not to be tied by any laws,' but freedom of men under government is to have a standing rule to live by, common to every one of that society, and made by the legislative power erected in it. It is a liberty to follow my own will in all things where that rule prescribes not, not to be subject to that inconstant, uncertain, unknown, arbitrary will of another man. . . ." (John Locke)

9. "Nothing could so far advance the cause of freedom as for state officials throughout the land to assert their rightful claims to lost state power; and for the federal government to withdraw promptly and totally from every jurisdiction which the constitution reserved to the states." (Barry Goldwater)

II

SEMANTICS: *Connotation*

In discussing denotation we covered what we normally think of as the *meaning* of a word; but denotation is seldom the whole story. "Lot" and "homesite" might refer to the same patch of ground, and yet a realtor might regard the latter word as more enticing and thus better suited to his purposes. The words "booze" and "liquor" designate the same fluid, but they do not at all have the same impact on the hearer or reader. What makes the difference in each case is that area of meaning called *connotation,* by which we mean the feelings and associations that cluster around all but a very few neutral, sterile words. Connotation cannot always be adequately covered by dictionaries, for it is a shifting, vague area of meaning which does not lend itself to sharp definition. Sometimes, for example, connotations are personal or local (the word "Yankee" would have very different connotations in New England and in the South). But most connotations are commonly associated with their words by enough people so that communication of feeling can take place. For, consciously or unconsciously, we express our feelings about the world through connotations; to use a word with a certain connotation is to pass judgment on the thing designated. If we are sensitive to connotations we can better express our own feelings, we can better appreciate the skillful handling of connotation in literature, and we can be on our guard against allowing our opinions to be molded against our better judgment by the impact of emotional language. "Speech in its essence is not neutral," says Kenneth Burke; "it is intensely moral—its names for objects contain the emotional overtones which give us the cues as to how we should act toward those objects."

To be sure, a word often evokes certain feelings only because of our attitudes toward the *object* being designated. It is natural that the terms "brainwash" and "concentration camp" should have unpleasant overtones, since the things themselves are thoroughly unpleasant. The words "Quaker" (meaning literally one who quakes) and "Methodist" (meaning a person of methodical habits) were originally mocking nicknames bestowed on those religious groups by their critics and carried derogatory associations; but once the organizations themselves had gained respectability, the terms became simply the names of the organizations and lost their original derisive meanings: at each stage, the feelings evoked by the words were conditioned by prevailing attitudes toward the *thing* being designated.

But in much connotation, feelings are suggested more by *words* than things. As we have already noted, we frequently find more than one word for the same object, each one suggesting a different range of feelings, so that the feelings seem to belong to the word rather than to the object itself. "Foam suggests the sea, froth suggests beer," says Fowler; it would be hard to describe objectively how foam differs from froth. A young girl would rather be called "slim" (or better "svelte") than "skinny." In dealing with the unpleasant facts of life, we are fond of manufacturing *euphemisms*—neutral or pleasant-sounding terms that some-how do not arouse the feelings that naturally go with the object. So to die becomes to "pass away," a prison becomes a "reformatory" or even a "home," old people become "senior citizens," inferior students become "exceptional learners," and the school principal in the *New Yorker* cartoon reassuringly tells the anxious parent, "There's no such thing as a bad boy. Hostile, perhaps. Aggressive, recalcitrant, destructive, even sadistic. But not *bad*." It is as if we thought we could magically change the nature of the object by changing the name it bears.

Connotation and Special Vocabularies

Some words take all or part of their connotation from the circumstances of use; slang terms, illiterate or dialect forms may have somewhat disagreeable or comic connotations because they are associated with the lower levels of society. Many slang terms seem to exist to express irreverent or unorthodox feelings and are perhaps called slang because they are felt as subversive not only of good English but of standard moral values as well. If someone calls the church a "gospel factory," the minister a "hallelujah peddler," and the members "amen-snorters," he is probably not very pious; if he calls his wife a "ball-and-chain," a "help-spend," or a "loud speaker," he has probably a rather cynical view of marriage. Such terms as "eye burner," "grade grabber," and "greasy grind" do not sound as if they had been invented by the members of Phi Beta Kappa. If such a slang term undergoes promotion and becomes part of the standard vocabulary, it is likely to shed its picturesque connotations in the process.

At the opposite extreme from slang, we have formal

vocabularies whose use is reserved for special topics and occasions. It is natural for an English-speaking Protestant to resort, in religious services, to the vocabulary and rhythms of the King James Bible and the Book of Common Prayer.

Man that is born of a woman, hath but a short time to live and is full of misery. He cometh up, and is cut down like a flower; he fleeth as it were a shadow, and never continueth in one stay.

In the midst of life we are in death: of whom may we seek for succour but of thee, O Lord, who for our sins art justly displeased? (The Burial of the Dead)

Generations of use have given this basically fine language an additional magic, and more modern translations of scripture are likely to seem somewhat flat by comparison, however valuable they may be in communicating to the reader untrained in Elizabethan English the plain sense of the text.

Metaphor

Slang is likely to be metaphorical; and in general metaphor is one of the most effective devices for extending connotation when, in poetry or some other context which demands concentration and the precise expression of emotion, we wish to express a feeling that has not become attached to any of the words normally used to describe the object we are discussing. The metaphor, we remember, is a condensed simile; we call one object by the name of another, meaning not that they are identical but that there is some significant point of comparison. "House of God" not only names a church but suggests the divine presence the worshiper feels there; "family tree" suggests not only the branching form which the genealogy takes on paper but also the ideas of growth and strength; "ship of state" (for government) suggests the ideas of order and subordination, of striving toward a goal, of courage in the face of danger. Metaphor is, in fact, one of the chief means by which language grows.

Control of Connotation

The control of connotation is particularly important in artistic works, but the problem has likewise its grossly practical side. All too many writers and speakers tend to confuse the communication of information with the expression of feeling. Writers of advertising are notoriously skillful at this sort of thing. The slogan "pure as the tear that falls upon a sister's grave" pretended to describe the quality of a brand of port wine, but if interpreted literally is not very complimentary; what the advertiser hoped to accomplish was to get an uncritical, sentimental response to emotionally charged words like "pure" and "sister" and somehow attach these emotional responses to his product, however remote the actual connection between wine and a deceased sister. It is possible to talk at considerable length without doing much more than play with emotions.

The progress of mankind can be traced by the progress of woman. Motherhood is part of the plan of the universe. The Mother is the fountain-head of the family, whose waters sweeten and purify. She has been the bulwark ever standing between civilization and barbarism. There is no language that can describe a Mother's love. It reigns eternal, knowing no limit. It reaches from earth to heaven. It is one of the sublime mysteries. The Mother is the uncrowned queen of the centuries who rules mankind and radiates the light that never fails. As a nation we spend three times as much for liquor as for education, and the only attitude to take in such adverse circumstances is to remember that the one constant factor is the love of a Mother for her children.

This quotation may seem extreme, but it is composite put together from actual phrases out of a number of "declamations."

The problem is especially complex when we deal with *value words*—words like "good," "evil," "lovely," "pretty," "useful," "elegant," and the like, whose principal function is to indicate the approval or disapproval of the speaker. By some writers such words are regarded as purely emotive —as "snarl" and "purr" words which do nothing but indicate an attitude. Generally, however, such words can be regarded as at least vaguely descriptive; they say or imply that a thing has certain characteristics and that as a consequence it merits our approval or disapproval. Even "good," one of the most general of our value words, can be concrete in context: we have a fair idea of what is meant by a good used car, or the long-dreamed-of good five-cent cigar, or even Perelman's good five-cent psychiatrist. A good doctor cures the sick and a good lawyer wins cases— the context makes the specific meaning clear. Many value words, such as "chaste," "blasphemous," "neat," "helpful," are quite descriptive. If value words were not descriptive, we should not need so many of them; a small set, expressing various grades of approval or disapproval, would be enough. (Some people of limited imagination do manage to get along with a few words like "nice," "lousy," or "cool.") In using such words we want to select the term which most exactly describes both the object and our feeling.

Unhappily value words are not always used either carefully or without design, the misuse being especially common in politics and advertising. Certain words often used
in controversy become after a while so charged with emotion that they are, in Hayakawa's phrase, "loaded," and
hence dangerous to use, even when in origin fairly descriptive; at least one should be on one's guard when one
hears them in controversy. Political terms such as "socialist," "Communist," "fascist," or even "totalitarian" are
capable of moderately exact definition in terms of party
membership or acceptance of a particular belief: neither
the socialist nor his enemy doubts that he believes in
"public ownership of the means of production." Terms
like "liberal" and "conservative" are harder to define because they are essentially relative, like "large" and "small,"
and change with the times, so that today's "conservative" is
a conservative because he holds to the beliefs of the nine-
teenth-century liberal; and yet among careful users in
proper context the terms are informative. But all these
terms are used more often than not as mere terms of praise
or abuse, so that a man may qualify as a socialist for wanting cheap electrical power and as a fascist for opposing
racketeering in labor. Fluoridation, health insurance, de-
segregation—all pass for "Communist plots" in the language of modern political oratory. Even words fairly
neutral and innocent in themselves may become loaded in
certain contexts; modern worship of science makes the
term attractive, and hence we get such phrases as "scientific grammar" and "scientific criticism" to designate
studies that could not possibly apply the true scientific
method to their purposes nor attain the mathematical exactitude of the physical sciences. A "people's democracy"

is likely to be a dictatorship. The cheapest and hence most standardized model of one contemporary automobile used to be called "Custom," though "custom" ought to refer to something made to order; the corresponding model of another make was called "Plaza," suggestive of fine hotels and limousines. All this is innocent enough, since no one buys a car sight unseen, but the orator who calls his mildly conservative opponent a "fascist" is far from innocent.

Slanting

So far we have been considering connotation with reference to single words and phrases, but there is also what we might call the *connotation of the whole,* the emotional import of the whole passage, which is not merely the sum total of the connotations, but the result of the complex interaction of the material presented, the vocabulary, and even such subtle qualities as sentence rhythm. Here as always we, as writers, must be careful to give exactly the feeling we wish to convey, and as readers we must avoid being improperly influenced by the artful manipulation of language. Let us take the following passage from Thorstein Veblen:

As it finds expression in the life of the barbarian, prowess manifests itself in two main directions—force and fraud. In varying degrees these two forms of expression are similarly present in modern warfare, in the pecuniary occupations, and in sports and games. Both lines of aptitudes are cultivated and strengthened by the life of sport as well as by the more serious forms of emulative life. Strategy or cunning is an element invariably present in games, as also in warlike pursuits and in the chase. In all of these employments strategy tends to develop into finesse and chicane. Chicane, falsehood, browbeating, hold a well-secured place in the method of procedure of any athletic contest and in games generally. The habitual employment of an umpire, and the minute technical regulations governing the limits and details of permissible fraud and strategic advantage, sufficiently attest the fact that fraudulent practices and attempts to overreach one's opponents are not adventitious features of the game. In the nature of the case habituation to sports should conduce to a fuller development of the aptitude for fraud; and the prevalence in the community of the predatory temperament which inclines men to sports connotes a prevalence of sharp practice and callous disregard of the interests of others, individually and collectively. Resort to fraud, in any guise and under any legitimation of law or custom, is an expression of a narrowly self-regarding habit of mind. It is needless to dwell at any length on the economic value of this feature of the sporting character.[1]

What this passage says in effect is that since both force and strategy are necessary for success in war, business, and sport, sport is a good preparation for business. This proposition (except for the implication that force is commonly used in business) is one that many businessmen and most coaches would applaud, yet it is expressed in such a way as to make both business and sport seem not only evil but a little ridiculous. For the strategy which is a perfectly legitimate part of most competitive games, Veblen uses extremely derogatory terms—"fraud," "chicane," "falsehood," "sharp practice." Skill in play becomes "aptitude for fraud"; the umpire instead of enforcing fair play, settles "the limits and details of permissible fraud"; and an interest in sports shows a "predatory temperament." If we can analyze such passages and can distinguish clearly between the information conveyed and the tone which has been given to the facts by the use of words having certain connotations, we shall be better able to protect ourselves from improper verbal influences.

[1] Thorstein Veblen, *The Theory of the Leisure Class*, New York, 1931, pp. 273–274.

This process by which an emotional tone is given to facts in order to influence the reader's attitude is aptly called *slanting*. With sufficient ingenuity, one can do remarkable tricks with facts and give a completely false impression without stating any outright falsehood. Here is a British description of the battles of Lexington and Concord:

. . . The Troops now combated with fresh Ardour, & marched in their return with undaunted countenances, receiving Sheets of fire all the way for many Miles, yet having no visible Enemy to combat with, for they never would face 'em in an open field, but always skulked & fired from behind Walls, & trees, & out of Windows of Houses, but this cost them dear for the Soldiers entered those dwellings, & put all the Men to death. Lord Percy has gained great honor by the conduct thro' this day of severe Service he was exposed to the hottest of the fire & animated the Troops with great coolness & spirit. Several officers are wounded & about 100 soldiers. The killed amount to near 50, as to the Enemy we can have no exact acct. but it is said there was about ten times the Number of them engaged, & that near 1000 of 'em have fallen.

Except for the exaggeration of the Colonial casualties, the details here are accurate enough, but one gets the impression that the "return" of the troops to their refuge in Boston was a victory of some kind. Notice, for instance, how much more of the passage is concerned with the courage of the troops than is concerned with the outcome of the action, and how the Colonists' prudence in fighting from shelter becomes "skulking."

Conclusions

One should avoid the easy position that the use of language to arouse or control emotion is dangerous and that as far as possible we ought to limit ourselves and others to the neutral expression of verifiable facts. Modern logicians have in fact managed to escape from emotional language through the use of symbolic logic, a kind of algebra of propositions. But we can hardly hope to escape from emotion in our everyday use of words, no matter how much we sharpen our perception of connotations. Nor would we wish to escape; having feelings, we wish to express them, get others to share them, even at times to impose them on others. We should not wish to violate reason or morality in our use of words. We shall always reject this sort of thing:

Can we endure four more years of political cannibalism at the hands of a predatory, power-hungry conglomeration of third-rate bosses and bureaucrats who can only stay in power by buying the votes of the nonproductive elements in society? Can we put up with a moron government whose stupidity, rigidity, and cupidity are leading us to the abyss of totalitarian tyranny?

But what about this?

With malice toward none; with charity for all; with firmness in the right as God gives us to see the right, let us strive on to finish the work we are in; to bind up the nation's wounds; to care for him who shall have borne the battle, and for his widow, and his orphan—to do all which may achieve and cherish a just and lasting peace among ourselves, and with all nations.

Surely we regard the sentiments from Lincoln's Second Inaugural Address as worthy ones; surely we would wish that more people in Reconstruction days had been moved by his rhetoric. Insofar as feeling is a legitimate part of human life, it is necessarily a part of language. And just so far as we strive in other areas to make feeling subservient to reason and law, just so far do we strive to control emotional language. A knowledge of semantics and of the kindred discipline of rhetoric can help us to exercise this control; and it is no flaw in the disciplines themselves if they can be utilized by a Hitler as well as a Lincoln.

Exercises in Connotation

EXERCISE A

Analyze the following value words in terms of their descriptive elements (or denotations) and the attitudes they imply.

Generous, thrifty, aggressive, kind, righteous, self-righteous, bestial, coarse, uncouth, immoral, unlawful, vicious, loathsome, horrible, hideous, charming, pretty, beautiful, charitable, efficient, interesting, brilliant.

EXERCISE B

Discuss the connotations and (if possible) the denotations of the following terms as used in political controversy. Write a grammatical fifty-word paragraph using as many of them as possible.

Union-baiter, do-gooder, reactionary, Wall Street, brainwashing, red-tinged, our forefathers, inflated profits, economic royalist, bureaucrat, thought control, socialized, cancerous growth, security, independence, rugged individualism, collectivist, deficit, thrift, monopoly, vested interests, discouraging initiative, smear, senior citizen, honest toil, exploitation, commiesymp, welfarism, neutralist, confiscation, extremist, featherbedding, egalitarian, bleeding heart, constitutional.

EXERCISE C

For each of the following words, give a word or phrase with approximately the same denotation but a different connotation (such as "scholar" for "pedant," "patriot" for "jingo," "individualist" for "queer").

Bohemian, prig, hick, eccentric, demagogue, cynic, mediocrity, brat, mossback, nonconformist, politician, criticism, fun-loving, sophistication, egghead.

EXERCISE D

Discuss the use of emotional words in the following passages. Try rephrasing some of the passages, keeping to the facts but implying an attitude or feeling different from that of the original. (See for example the restatement of Veblen's ideas on page 35.)

1. I know in my heart that I'm not a liar. I'm just a prevaricator.

2. "We have gone down Pragmatic Lane to the mire of 'no valid values,' where technology, disembowelled of compassion and eased of any discipline of wisdom, is taught in mechanic pride and spiritual sloth with a diploma guaranteed by democratic process." (*Modern Age*)

3. "The anti-sexual emphasis of early Christianity came partly from the Orient, where certain ascetic cults glorified celibacy, masochism and dirt, and thus gave lazy men of that time a chance to escape from family responsibility without condemnation." (Paul Blanshard)

4. "This is social levelling, wherein the crushing weight of the State would flatten, smooth and make of all humanity a sort of gluey mixture, boiling over the fires of other men's passions, poured into moulds, preformed, predigested and predestined to the conformity of an ant hill." (Robert J. Needles)

5. "Whenever we buy such goods [goods sold at less than the cost of producing them] remember we are stealing somebody's labor. Don't let us mince the matter. I say, in plain Saxon, STEALING—taking from him the proper reward of his work, and putting it into your own pocket. You know well enough that the thing could not have been offered you at that price, unless distress of some kind had forced the producer to part with it.

. . . The old barons of the middle ages used, in general, the thumbscrew to extort property; we moderns use, in preference, hunger or domestic affliction: but the fact of extortion remains precisely the same." (John Ruskin)

6. "As usual, the employers' spokesmen attempt to use soothing syrup to sweet-talk the public into believing that they are not greedy and are not attempting to have the producers subsidize the coupon clippers through substandard wages and substandard conditions." (Union Agent)

7. ". . . There is about as much danger of the establishment of religion in this country as there is of the return of sanity to the Supreme Court. The neurotic Mrs. M_____ who brought the action to impose a silence on the subject of God on all the children of the United States who study in public schools, because her moon-faced son's rights are otherwise trampled upon, was the perfect plaintiff, poetically speaking, for this case." (*National Review*)

8. "The movie is the diversion of slaves, the pastime of illiterate wretches harried by wants and worries, the astutely poisoned pabulum of a multitude condemned by the forces of Moloch to this vile degradation." (Georges Duhamel)

Exercise E

Write an essay analyzing the verbal technique of some essay, article, or speech which shows an obvious use (or misuse) of emotional language.

III

LOGIC: *Introduction*

Even for the most skeptical, belief is an absolute necessity for practical existence. At the very least, we have to have faith that the material world will continue in its accustomed ways, that tomorrow as today iron will be hard and clay soft, that objects will continue to fall toward the earth instead of flying off into the sky. Without belief, action would be paralyzed; we should never know what to do in a given situation. What distinguishes the rational from the irrational thinker is not the presence or absence of belief, but the grounds on which belief is accepted; and what distinguishes the convincing from the unconvincing argument is the degree to which the writer can show that his beliefs are worthy of acceptance.

There are some sources of belief which are either absolutely unsound or to be resorted to only when all other methods fail. A hunch is not an absolutely useless guide, because it may be based on knowledge which has temporarily slipped our minds, but we should be foolish to restrict ourselves to a hunch when pertinent evidence is available. Our casual impression of a prospective employee may be useful, but full knowledge of his previous record is more valuable. Tradition may be a proper guide in some areas of life, but we cannot accept witchcraft or even Newtonian physics merely because our forefathers did. All too often we believe simply because we want to believe. It is comforting to think that "there is always room at the top," or that "there are no atheists in fox-holes," or that "football makes good citizens." But such beliefs are the most treacherous of all beliefs, because we tend to protect them by ignoring contrary evidence until at some crisis the brute facts force themselves on our attention. A groundless belief is not merely wrong morally; it is an unsafe guide to conduct.

What then are the legitimate sources of belief? In a scientific age we instinctively answer, evidence or investigation. We believe that a worker is reliable because we have seen him at work frequently over a considerable period of time; we believe that a certain remedy will cure a certain disease because trained observers have watched its operation in a large number of cases (here, as often, we have to trust the reports of others' investigations); we believe that haste makes waste because we have seen it happen so many times. Having observed that a certain number of instances of the phenomenon have a certain character, we infer that other instances of the same kind will have the same character. Such a process of generalizing from particulars is known as *induction*. Somewhat less common (at least in its more ambitious forms) is *deduction*. Where induction puts facts together to get ideas or *generalizations*, deduction puts ideas together to discover what other ideas can be inferred from them. If we know that John is the son of David and that David is the son of William, we see immediately that John must be the grandson of William—there can be no possible doubt, and there is no need for investigation. If a student must pass composition in order to graduate, and Mr. X has not yet passed it, then Mr. X cannot yet graduate. In each case, provided only that the first two ideas or *premises* are true, then the third—the conclusion—must likewise be true. If one is willing to agree that the premises are sound, one will be forced to agree with the conclusion.

In every mind there will be a few beliefs which cannot be proved either by induction or deduction: basic standards of value, ultimate articles of faith, matters of inner conviction which we would be hard put to prove but without which we could scarcely think or act. Religious principles might be thought of as the most obvious example, but philosophy and even science exhibit the same necessity. In plane geometry we must begin with the axioms and postulates from which the rest of the system is deduced. It is an article of faith that "things equal to the same thing are equal to each other"; we must believe it or give up plane geometry. Similarly, virtually all induction and hence all scientific conclusions and practically all action depend on a faith in the uniformity of nature—that the laws of matter will be the same tomorrow as today. It seems only common sense to assume that water will continue to freeze at 32° Fahrenheit hereafter, but there is no way of proving the assumption.

Induction and deduction are not exclusively the tools of the philosopher and the scientist, but in rough-and-ready half-conscious forms are part of the everyday thought processes of all rational human beings, however limited their education. It is not infrequently argued that logic in the more formal sense is neither necessary nor useful for human life, since common or horse sense can serve us far better in practical affairs. Such an argument involves a half truth. In the first place, we might question whether logic and common sense are really so different. If common sense has any value, it is because it is based on experience, and hence on some process of conscious or unconscious generalizing. What really distinguishes common sense from logic is that it tends to take short cuts: it seldom bothers to work out all the steps in the argument. Certain processes work in our brains, and we acquire a sudden conviction that something is true. It is fortunate that we have common sense and intuition to depend on, for time does not always allow us to work things out logically or go hunting for evidence. It is certainly better to investigate a prospective employee thoroughly, but if we have to fill the job on the spot, we shall have to trust our impressions of his character. Very rarely (if we are wise) we may even trust our common sense in preference to what seems to be scientific evidence. Many a parent or teacher has finally nerved himself to go against the "scientific findings" of a child psychologist or educator. (But perhaps what is wrong here is not really science but its interpretation by incompetent individuals.) Whole areas of human decision lie outside of the range of logic and sometimes even of common sense. One may be able to prove by critical principles that a book has every virtue that belongs to a masterpiece, and the book may in fact be quite unreadable. Cold reason cannot rule all areas of human life. It is useless to tell a young man that a certain girl has all the qualifications of an ideal wife if he happens to detest her. Nevertheless, to scorn logic and hold to horse sense is a dangerous business. An appeal to common sense all too often represents an attempt to evade the responsibility of looking at evidence or working out the problem rationally. Common sense sometimes tells people peculiar things about such matters as family life and racial and economic problems. To come down to the practical problem of communication, our personal intuitions are probably of very little interest to our readers or listeners, however much they value their own. What they expect from us is logic and evidence.

By its very nature, logic deals in statements or *propositions;* they are the materials of deductive reasoning and the products of inductive reasoning. By a proposition we mean a group of words of which it can be said that it is either true or false. (Even if it is false, it is still a proposition.) Not all sentences are propositions. A question or command is not a proposition; we cannot say that "Who is there?" is true or that "Do your homework!" is false. A proposition is roughly equivalent to the grammarian's *declarative sentence,* though not exactly equivalent, since a declarative sentence might contain several different propositions ("The sky is blue, and the grass is green") or express what is really a question or command ("The audience will leave quietly").

Furthermore, it is important to make a clear-cut distinction between a proposition that is merely factual and one that implies a *judgment.* "He served at Valley Forge" and "He was a loyal soldier" are both statements, but not of the same kind. The first is a matter of fact: either he served or he did not, and there is the possibility at least of proving the matter one way or another to the satisfaction of all. The second is a little different: since the word "loyal" implies praise for something, it passes a judgment. Another person, fully informed of the same facts, might disagree because of a differing conception of what constitutes loyalty; absolute proof one way or another is impossible, since an element of personal feeling will always intrude. "Fact" here means "a piece of verifiable information"; that which makes statements factual is the quality that makes them susceptible of conclusive proof through careful empirical observation. "Columbus died in 1491" and "Martians have six legs" are in this sense factual, though the one statement is known to be false and the other is at present impossible of verification; neither statement implies praise or blame, and, given sufficient evidence in the form of documents or specimen Martians, either could be proved true or false to the satisfaction of all reasonable people. "George Washington was loyal" still involves a judgment, however much the statement may be confirmed by evidence and however universally it may be believed. A British writer in 1776 might plausibly have called Washington disloyal, and given his point of view, it is hard to see how we should ever have been able to reach an agreement with him. True, the distinction between facts and judgments is not always simple or clear-cut. The statement "He is intelligent" certainly contains an element of judgment; yet it is susceptible of confirmation by means of standard tests and might in some contexts be considered factual. For further illustration of the distinction, compare the following pairs of sentences; in each case, the first sentence is factual, and the second implies a judgment.

She has a 36–26–36 figure.
She is shapely.

He has been sentenced to a ten-year term in the penitentiary.
He is a criminal.

He has written five books which were published by university presses and favorably reviewed.
He is an eminent scholar.

Needless to say, judgments are not to be condemned; they are merely to be recognized for what they are. It may not always be easy to do this. When the educator says, "The learner cannot be considered aside from his environment," he seems to be stating a factual generalization. But a little reflection reminds us that, rightly or wrongly, pupils are often judged without reference to their environment, and that to make sense the sentence must read, "The learner *ought not* to be considered aside from his environment," a form which clearly identifies it as a judgment. "Good children brush their teeth" has the form of a generalization and might actually represent the result of investigation on the dental habits of children known to be "good." Probably, however, it is a judgment, telling how the speaker thinks children ought to behave; and in a certain context the sentence might amount to a command. What is important is to make our meaning clear in the first place, and to show our readers that our evaluations have been rational. Judgments may be supported by evidence and argument; they need not be mere emotional reactions. The statement "He was loyal" can be supported by a definition of loyalty and instances of loyal conduct.

It goes without saying that we cannot work logically with a statement that does not have intellectual content. We should try to avoid those statements, all too common in controversy, which do nothing more than express feeling or prejudice. The following is technically a valid argument:

No-good rats should be hung.
X is a no-good rat.
Therefore, X should be hung.

But we should hope that no jury would follow such reasoning. Emotive statements, such as were discussed under connotation, are utterly out of place in logic. Nothing can be deduced from a feeling.

Exercise in Propositions

Indicate whether each of the following sentences is a proposition or not. If it is a proposition, indicate whether it is factual or implies a judgment. If the sentence shows characteristics of both, distinguish factual from emotional elements.

1. Many people would regard gum chewing as even less desirable than cigarette smoking.
2. The main lesson in school is how to get along with others.
3. The moon is made of green cheese.
4. Socialism presupposes a far greater equality and uniformity of capacity and merit than actually exists among human beings.
5. Socialism proposes to interfere with the freedom of the individual to whatever extent the sovereign may dictate.
6. "Defense measures will not, and often should not, be held within the limits that bind civil authority in peace." (U.S. Supreme Court)
7. Not to quarrel is unhealthy.
8. He has always wanted to own a large, elegant dog.
9. Psychologists aren't sure why women pick fights in the kitchen.
10. "I am prepared under my constitutional duty to recommend the measures that a stricken nation in the midst of a stricken world may require." (Franklin D. Roosevelt)
11. "Communism relies upon terror and oppression, a controlled press and radio, fixed elections, and the suppression of personal freedom." (Harry S Truman)
12. In our land men are equal, but they are free to be different.
13. Pumpkins are a good source of Vitamin A.

14. The president's philosophy is in the tradition of Goering, who said that common good comes before individual good.
15. India has pressing problems of overpopulation, disease, and hunger.
16. As a gesture to frugality, anti-spending congressmen put up a fight every time a new debt limit is proposed.
17. The forces of bigotry have tyrannized the men and women of goodwill.
18. Physical fitness is a great thing.
19. He has shown a congenital preference for weak compromises in critical situations.
20. Railroad spokesmen said negotiations with the five operating units had broken down.
21. "Ain't" is "a vulgar contraction of the negative phrases *am not* and *are not.*" (*Century Dictionary*)
22. "Ain't" is "used orally in most parts of the U.S. by many educated speakers." (*Webster's Third New International Dictionary*)
23. "Skyhawk 'E' has a payload of 8,000 pounds of offensive and defensive weapons. . . . Its stall speed of 94 knots— lowest of any combat jet—gives it unmatched low-level maneuverability." (Advertisement)
24. Americans are inclined to be too blunt in their dealings with foreigners.
25. Rising teen-age unemployment constitutes an indictment of our society.

IV

LOGIC: *Induction*

Induction has already been defined as the process by which we generalize from particulars; usually, we have said, it involves the assumption that particular events encountered in the future will be like those we have encountered in the past. There are, as it happens, some examples of perfect induction, that is, generalizations which do not involve any element of prediction, because all the possible examples of the type have been examined. "All members of the present class passed the examination" might be such an example of perfect induction, provided we have actually checked the grade of every student. "Honor high school graduates do well in college" is a different sort of generalization, for we can hardly have examined the future cases or even all the possible past cases. Yet, in using such generalizations, we often expect that unexamined past as well as future cases will tend to confirm the generalization. At the same time we allow for the possibility of exceptions at all times, and even for the possibility that in the future changing circumstances may invalidate the whole generalization. The statement is sufficiently probable so that an admissions officer could act on it, but it is far from certain.

That inductive generalizations are probable rather than

certain is a truth that we no doubt recognize clearly enough from our experience with the common-sense generalizations of everyday life. We have enough faith in the notion that dogs are friendly or tigers are dangerous to avoid the latter and pet the former, but we know that there is nothing immutable about the propositions: some dogs are dangerous, and tigers are occasionally tamed. The propositions of science, at least of the physical sciences, would seem on the other hand to be not merely probable but in some cases absolutely certain. Who would question the freezing point of water or the atomic weight of gold? But even scientific generalizations possess only an unusually high degree of probability and not absolute certainty. Scientific theories are in a continual state of revision. Newton's "laws" of gravitation once seemed eternal truth, but they have been revised or superseded by other theories. For practical purposes, the layman may well accept scientific statements as certain, but the knowledge that an inductive generalization never really gets beyond a high degree of probability may give him a healthy skepticism toward the generalizations he deals with in everyday life. In practice it is usually not dangerous to speak of true and false generalizations, but it would be more accurate to speak of degrees of probability or improbability.

Sources of Evidence

Induction is generalization from evidence; manifestly we ought not to generalize without evidence that is both authentic in character and sufficient in quantity. The question of the authenticity of the evidence can be very simple or very complex. The sources of evidence can be virtually comprehended under the categories of *observation* and *authority*. Sometimes, in other words, the evidence comes from our own observations, either casual or systematic. Having been repeatedly pleased with the purchases made at a certain store, we reasonably infer that goods bought there will be satisfactory. This is a casual, common-sense inference. At the other extreme we have the operations of science, in which the evidence is collected through elaborate, repeated, and carefully controlled experiments. It might seem as if we could always depend on our own observations, but unhappily our senses and memories often deceive us, as the confusion of witnesses in court trials depressingly illustrates. Even in science errors of observation, though carefully guarded against, are not entirely unknown. A reputable scientist *thought* he had overthrown Einstein on the basis of some measurements of the speed of light which no other experimenter was ever able to duplicate. There is always the danger that we will see only what we want to see, even though the error may not be deliberate. A bigot with a deep prejudice against a racial or religious group will manage to notice and remember incidents where members of the group behave badly and pass over those where they behave well. The questionnaire is an important tool in some kinds of investigation; but unless a questionnaire is carefully worded it may obtain erroneous results—the way a question is asked may predispose to a certain kind of answer. A group of good students asked "Do you cheat frequently?" might hesitate to answer at all, since even a "no" might leave the impression that they did *some* cheating. Suppose that we were to take a poll on the appearance of controversial speakers on college campuses, and that we were to frame the question thus: "Should radicals and subversives be allowed to use college assemblies as platforms to propagate their ideas?" Except among the most liberal, the answer would probably be "no." Suppose, however, that the question were put as follows: "Should students be allowed to hear champions of unpopular views as part of their educational experience?" Then we might expect a more favorable response. Observation is in fact an art, and we must always be able to demonstrate that the evidence has been gathered in a way that does not affect the results.

Of course most of the information we work with in academic matters, especially student papers, does not derive from direct observation but from indirect sources, especially books. The use of secondhand information constantly raises the question of authority: how far are we justified in believing the learned lecture or the printed page? In general we expect to depend on authorities who are competent in the field. We naturally trust the man who is discussing his own field of study and distrust the man who claims to speak in an area where he has no special qualifications. There are doubtless incautious people who really accept movie stars as authorities on tobacco and baseball players as authorities on diet, but wiser thinkers remember that men as great as Henry Ford and Thomas Edison possessed some surprising beliefs: Ford was aggressively ignorant of history and Edison had some odd ideas about gravity. In the end we usually have to accept the weight of the received opinions of the body of experts in the field. A quack may loudly proclaim that his cancer cure is being suppressed by a conspiracy of the American Medical Association, but an intelligent patient will take the word of the doctors. Even the authority of George Bernard Shaw, who was opposed to vaccination, cannot outweigh the pronouncements of the whole medical profession. If a novelist claims to have found a way to detect water underground or a minister a way to find oil (and such things have happened), we should do well to question their training in geology.

Even where there is no question of the authenticity of the authority, certain precautions are in order. One concerns date. In some areas, especially science, authorities may become obsolete very rapidly; Darwin no longer provides the last word on evolution, nor Freud on psychoanalysis. Another concerns bias. Labor leaders and businessmen are undoubtedly experts of a sort on economic problems, but their particular economic interests would keep them from having the impartiality of an economics professor. Even the latter might display a bias derived not from self-interest but from adherence to some particular school of economic thought, so that it would be well to check his conclusions against those of other authorities.

Adequacy of Evidence

The problem of the adequacy of evidence is complicated, since our ideas of adequacy vary according to the peculiarities of the problem and the kind of investigation required. We could imagine situations in which a single piece of evidence would be sufficient to establish a generalization, if not with absolute certainty (which is impossible anyway), then with a high degree of probability. We would have to be dealing with phenomena whose operations were regular, to be sure that the example was absolutely typical, and to be careful not to draw a broader generalization than was warranted. If we once succeeded in dissolving gold in aqua regia, we should assume that we could do it again, since chemical reactions seem to obey certain "laws"; although, because of the possibility that chance factors such as impurities or variations in temperature might operate, a careful scientist would be anxious to accumulate instances before making a pronouncement. If a student produces a good theme, we can safely say that he is capable of writing well, but this does not assure us that he will always do so. Generally speaking, the more evidence available, the more convincing the conclusions, since the likelihood of a chance factor is decreased. Statisticians have devised elaborate formulas for determining the number of instances needed in a given case; if, for instance, comparison were to be made of the performance of different groups of students taught by varying methods, we should probably not want to work with groups of less than one hundred.

Mere quantity, however, is insufficient. Instances prove nothing or next to nothing if the investigator has accumulated only the instances that confirm his theory and has ignored the contradictory examples. We do not prove that high school training in English is inadequate by pointing to the (admittedly considerable) number of incompetent writers in college classes; this number must be balanced against those who are competent. It is important, too, that by a process of *sampling* we make sure that the instances are typical and represent the proper range and cross section. If we are comparing two groups of one hundred students each, we must make sure that the two groups represent equal ability and that all the abler students do not turn up in one group. If one group was scheduled for class at eight o'clock and the other at eleven o'clock, for instance, there is at least the possibility that the time of day would affect the students' performance and thus the results of the investigation. If one wanted to get the average views of the student body on athletics, he would not merely poll the football team or the members of Phi Beta Kappa. Even a sizable dormitory might provide a misleading sample, since it would usually represent but a single sex and would contain few fraternity or sorority members. The students enrolled in a required course might seem to offer a random sample, provided that they were not drawn predominantly from a single year, as would be the case with freshman composition. It has been suggested, rightly or wrongly, that the Kinsey reports give a faulty impression of American sexual habits because only a rather uninhibited person would consent to be interviewed at all. Whether the top layer constitutes a typical sample of a box of berries will depend on the honesty of the farmer.

Analysis of Evidence: Descriptive Generalizations

It is convenient to distinguish empirical generalizations into those that are simply *descriptive* and those that involve *causal relations*. With descriptive generalizations it is usually sufficient to accumulate positive instances and consider the number and importance of negative instances. "Birds fly," "Stocks are gaining," "The weather has been pleasant this spring," are generalizations of this kind. Aside from the possibility of statistical error, trouble can arise through difficulties in interpreting the evidence. There is no question that middle-class school children generally score higher on intelligence tests than lower-class children; the question comes in trying to decide the significance of the evidence. In the first place, it is unlikely that a test can ever be devised to measure native intelligence with absolute accuracy; and in the second place, it is obviously impossible to design a test whose results will not be influenced to some degree by the child's previous training and environment. A person's IQ may fluctuate somewhat through the years, and scores on the tests may even be improved by coaching. Apparently, the difference in score between the social classes means something, but to determine what that something is requires considerable analysis and interpretation.[1]

Analysis of Evidence: Causal Relations

Induction may go beyond mere description to consider causal relations. To say that graduates of school A score a higher average on English tests than students in school B is merely to describe; to say that the higher scores of the students in school A were due to superior instruction is to ascribe a cause to the difference in marks. Most of the more troublesome inductive problems are causal. To begin with, the term "cause" is itself somewhat ambiguous. We might say of an unsatisfactory student that he was dropped from school because of poor grades; or because he had poor study habits; or because he had never been taught how to study. The poor grades are, of course, the immediate occasion for his leaving; poor study habits presumably explain the poor grades; poor instruction is supposed to explain the poor habits. Immediate and remote causes are always to be distinguished.

One of the most common errors in handling causal generalizations is conventionally labeled *post hoc ergo propter hoc* ("after this therefore because of this"), the error of as-

---

[1] For a fuller treatment of the point, see Martin Mayer, *The Schools*, New York, 1961, Chapters 5 and 6.

suming that one event causes another simply because it precedes it in time. From the fact that children generally (though by no means always) resemble their parents in intelligence, it seems natural to assume that intelligence is inherited; but the mere fact of resemblance is by no means conclusive. Children are usually brought up by their parents, and psychologists who believe that intelligence is determined by the environment can argue that children resemble their parents in intelligence because the parents dominate the early environment. Proof that intelligence is largely inherited had to be obtained by means other than the mere comparison of parents and children—for instance, by studying orphans in institutions, who have varying heredity but the same environment, and by comparing identical twins, who have identical genes, with fraternal twins, who have somewhat different mixtures of the parental genes.[2]

The fact that two phenomena constantly appear together does not necessarily indicate that one is the cause of the other. Statistics seem to show that business executives have large vocabularies, and unwary English teachers have sometimes suggested to their students that a large vocabulary might be a help to business success. The relationship may, however, be quite different; perhaps success causes the executive to acquire a large vocabulary through the variety of his business and social contacts, or success and vocabulary both may be the results of some other factor, such as intelligence or education. Complex phenomena may not be the result of any one single cause

[2] The discussion of this and associated problems in Chapter 4 of H. J. Eysenck's *Uses and Abuses of Psychology* (London, 1962) provides an excellent illustration of the pitfalls of induction.

but may arise from a combination of factors. From the fact that juvenile delinquency is less common in Italy than in the United States and that the Italian father is reputed to have more authority than the American father, a popular magazine concluded that lack of paternal authority was the sole cause of juvenile delinquency in the United States. A careful social scientist, even if he were willing to assume the stronger discipline of the Italian father, would want to consider what other factors might be operating. Even if two phenomena occur so frequently together that it seems safe to say that there is some causal connection, we should still have several possibilities to consider: that *A* caused *B*, that *B* caused *A*, or that both *A* and *B* were caused by some third factor. To feel sure that *A* caused *B*, we should not only observe that *B* regularly follows *A*, but we should make sure that there is no third factor *C* that constantly accompanies both.

Part of the art of induction lies in the accurate statement of conclusions, mainly in distinguishing between generalizations supposed to be universally true and those not intended to be more than generally true. In the physical sciences most generalizations have something like universal validity, but in the social sciences and certainly in common life they seldom have it. The two types can be clearly distinguished in terms of the effect of discovering an exception. A universal generalization would be overthrown by the discovery of a single clear exception, while a looser generalization would presumably stand as long as it proved true more often than not. Much trouble arises from forgetting that some generalizations are never meant to be one hundred percent accurate. During the McCarthy era and since, many politicians have seemed to operate on the assumption that all Communists are invariably spies and traitors, though the evidence could hardly be stretched to prove very much more than that a substantial number of Communists might reasonably be suspected of such activity. To avoid clumsiness we may state generalizations such as "Cows give milk" and "Babies cry" without naming all the qualifications and exceptions and special circumstances, but we need to keep in mind that such qualifications and exceptions do exist. To say that all *A* are *B* is emphatically not the same as saying that most *A* are *B* or that *A* tends to be *B*.

In practice, we rarely embark on an inductive study without some sort of preliminary or provisional theory. Instead of looking at phenomena simply with the idea of seeing what is there, we look to see whether an opinion we have tentatively adopted is confirmed. If not, we modify it or discard it in favor of a more promising theory. Tests would never have been conducted to establish a connection between tobacco and lung cancer if the suspicion had not already existed that there was such a connection.

The Hypothesis

A form of inference differing from the ordinary generalization is the *hypothesis*. By hypothesis is meant, in this context, a conjectured explanation for some phenomenon whose true cause cannot for the moment be discovered.[3] The process is that of working back from the known effect to the unknown cause. The sudden disappearance of the moon from the sky would lead us to assume that a

[3] The term is sometimes properly used to designate a tentative theory assumed for purposes of investigation. The two meanings are not always distinct.

cloud bank was passing even if we could not actually see the clouds as such; unless we assume the clouds, we would have no plausible explanation for the disappearance of the moon. Graphic—though, from a strictly logical point of view, often very unsound—examples of this kind of reasoning overflow in the average detective story. Here, for instance, is the celebrated Sherlock Holmes at work:

With a resigned air and a somewhat weary smile, Holmes begged the beautiful intruder to take a seat, and to inform us what it was that was troubling her.

"At least it cannot be your health," said he, as his keen eyes darted over her; "so ardent a bicyclist must be full of energy."

She glanced down in surprise at her own feet, and I observed the slight roughening of the side of the sole caused by the friction of the edge of the pedal.

"Yes, I bicycle a good deal, Mr. Holmes, and that has something to do with my visit to you to-day."

My friend took the lady's ungloved hand, and examined it with as close an attention and as little sentiment as a scientist would show to a specimen.

"You will excuse me, I am sure. It is my business," said he, as he dropped it. "I nearly fell into the error of supposing that you were typewriting. Of course, it is obvious that it is music. You observe the spatulate finger-ends, Watson, which is common to both professions? There is a spirituality about the face, however"—she gently turned it towards the light—"which the typewriter does not generate. This lady is a musician."

"Yes, Mr. Holmes, I teach music."

"In the country, I presume, from your complexion."

"Yes, sir, near Farnham, on the borders of Surrey."

In other words, since cycling could cause a roughened shoe, and playing the piano flatten the fingers, we conjecture that a person showing these effects is likely to be a cyclist and a musician. When Robinson Crusoe found the footprint on the shore, he had to assume the presence of another human being on the island in order to account for it; he had not seen that human being, but he was well justified in assuming his presence.

There are certain inherent difficulties in handling hypotheses. They tend to have only a fair degree of probability, since for every effect there are usually a number of different possible causes. Holmes himself acknowledged that typing might be the cause of his client's spatulate fingers and had to resort to the "spiritual look" (whatever that is) to prove her a musician. A policeman who found a man lying unconscious in the gutter outside a saloon might reasonably suppose alcohol to be the cause of the distress, but he would be grossly negligent if he did not consider illness or injury as possible explanations. It is part of the normal machinery of the detective story to tempt the reader into forming a false hypothesis and then to reveal the right one, quite unexpectedly, at the end.

Such considerations might lead us to despair of any kind of certainty in dealing with hypotheses, but the situation is by no means so desperate. In the first place, a hypothesis usually does have somewhat the status of a provisional theory which can be confirmed or overthrown by further investigation. Sherlock Holmes confirms his hypotheses by getting his client to acknowledge that she is indeed a cycling pianist from the country, and a doctor could establish whether the man in the gutter was ill or drunk. In science, systematic testing in the laboratory is the natural way out; if the conjectured cause can be made to produce the known effect regularly, the problem is solved.

There are times, of course, when the nature of the situation does not permit final confirmation, but even then we can at least look for degrees of probability. The man who feels drops of moisture falling from the sky assumes rain without stopping to consider the improbable possibility that a practical joker is showering him from a helicopter. The conduct of Hauptmann, who was executed for the Lindbergh kidnapping, could hardly be explained except on the assumption of his guilt: he spent some of the ransom money, the ladder used in the kidnapping was made from wood from his house, the ransom letters were in his handwriting, and the child's sleeping jacket was in his possession. Edmund Pearson, in discussing the Lindbergh case, mentions some other celebrated criminals who were also found in circumstances that only one reasonable hypothesis could explain: George Joseph Smith, three of whose wives (insured) drowned in the bathtub, and Dr. Crippen, who suddenly fled abroad with his typist, leaving fragments of his wife behind. Here are some remarks by Patrick Henry, spoken in 1775 with reference to military preparations made by Great Britain:

I ask gentlemen, sir, what means this martial array, if its purpose be not to force us to submission? Can gentlemen assign any other possible motive for it? Has Great Britain any enemy in this quarter of the world, to call for all this accumulation of navies and armies? No, sir, she has none. They are meant for us; they can be meant for no other.

The decision of the British government to undertake such extensive and expensive maneuvers required some explanation; war with another European power being apparently out of the question, Henry turned to the only other plausible hypothesis, that the armaments were intended to coerce the American colonies, and on this hypothesis he was prepared to act.

Aside from inherent plausibility, simplicity is likely to be the mark of a good hypothesis. We *can* explain the existence of Shakespeare's plays on the hypothesis that the playwright Christopher Marlowe, whom history records as having been murdered before many of the plays were produced, actually was spirited abroad, wrote the plays, and sent them back to England to be produced under Shakespeare's name. But the hypothesis that Shakespeare wrote his own plays is a good deal simpler and, considering the vanity of authors, inherently far more plausible. We can explain the teacher's presence in the classroom at the moment the bell rings by supposing that he is walking in his sleep and has arrived there by chance, but it is simpler to suppose that he is there to meet the class. It is possible to explain mental health programs as radical plots to undermine our faith in American sanity, but simpler to regard them as honest efforts to combat mental illness.

As a logical device hypothesis is susceptible to all kinds of abuses; careless or unscrupulous thinkers constantly offer us hypotheses which, without genuine confirmation, they regard as proved simply because the hypotheses explain phenomena, after a fashion. Some of the examples are merely comic, as is the case in the controversies over the authorship of Shakespeare's plays. Somewhat less comic was the furor over flying saucers. It may be true that the presence of Martian observers in saucer-shaped vehicles in our atmosphere would explain the fact that honest observers have seen objects of a certain shape and speed in the sky. But there is no real evidence for the existence of rational life on Mars, and the simpler and therefore more acceptable hypothesis would be that the observers were deceived by known phenomena such as weather balloons.

(Here we notice that, short of an actual landing by Martians, final confirmation is virtually impossible.) The saucer scare may be considered harmless, though it acquired a sinister aspect when the Air Force was accused of plotting to suppress evidence on the matter. It is characteristic of certain oversuspicious people to explain in terms of "plots" all sorts of things for which rational people find simpler and more plausible explanations. The old belief in witchcraft was in a sense a kind of hypothesis to explain such troublesome facts as sickness and crop failure, for which our ancestors simply did not possess the scientific explanations we accept today. Nor does the existence of an accepted scientific explanation necessarily deter some men from continuing to manufacture alternative hypotheses. To most of us, fossils in ancient rocks are evidence for the existence of organisms that lived eons ago, but the fossils have also been accounted for on the hypothesis that they were placed in the rocks by the devil to tempt unwary scientists into infidelity. Often we have to work with unproved hypotheses, but we should not put any more stock in them than necessary.

Conclusions

At its best, the process of induction exhibits all the rigors of scientific method. That ordinary expository essays, especially student essays, will always show such rigor is probably too much to expect, though a term paper might very well be a genuine exercise in systematic induction. Nonetheless, there are certain minimum standards of honesty and responsibility which any writer or speaker ought to meet. He can be cautious about offering ill-considered or implausible hypotheses; he can avoid inappropriate, or biased, or dated authorities; he can take pains in the analysis of causal relations. If he must work with a limited body of evidence, he can still attempt proper sampling, and he can admit the tentative nature of his conclusions. The world is perpetually engaged in the manufacture of hasty generalizations; we should do our best not to add to the supply.

Exercises in Induction

Exercise A

What evidence might be collected to support the following generalizations? What precautions (sampling, etc.) would be needed to guard against error in each case? Some of the propositions may not be capable of rigorous inductive proof.

1. Praise is a greater educational force than blame.
2. Students in social-living courses learn more than students in English courses.
3. "Many children slouch because of lack of self-confidence." (Dr. Spock)
4. A grade of 85 percent in school today is worth only as much as a grade of 60 percent twenty years ago.
5. Fraternities encourage college spirit.
6. Fraternities encourage conformity.
7. Comic books stimulate sadism and masochism.
8. Church attendance discourages juvenile delinquency.
9. Millions of people today are more adequately housed because of government housing programs.
10. The moral character of American society is changing.

Exercise B

Suggest one or more probable hypotheses to explain each of the following states of affairs.

1. An instructor meets his eight o'clock class as usual but fails to appear for his nine o'clock. His lecture notes for the

nine o'clock class are lying on his desk; his office door is open; his car is gone from the parking lot.

2. A student has been assigned a term paper on a specific topic; he is expected to submit an outline and note cards in advance. He submits neither outline nor note cards; at the last possible minute he produces an excellent paper which does not fit the assignment. (If he wrote an excellent final examination, how would this fact affect our hypothesis?)

3. A traveler in the Highlands of Scotland was entertained in a castle on the seacoast and was lodged in a chamber supposed to be haunted. During the night a ghostly figure appeared and for an hour watched him and refused to allow him to leave his bed. The traveler was a revenue officer; the district was notorious for smuggling. (After Sir Walter Scott)

4. A certain Archibald Fisher disappeared mysteriously, having been last seen in the company of three brothers, Archibald, Henry, and William Trailor, with the latter of whom he lived. William gave such an improbable account of the disappearance as to arouse suspicion of foul play. Henry suggested that his brothers had killed Fisher; he had, he said, seen them lift the body of a man into their wagon, and signs of struggle were found at the supposed scene of the crime. Later, however, a doctor from a neighboring town reported that Fisher was alive and lying ill at his house, whither Fisher had wandered in a state of derangement, a disorder to which he was subject as the result of a head injury suffered several years before. (After Abraham Lincoln)

5. A woman in a delirium mentioned the names of several deceased relatives and then the name of a relative supposed to be still alive. This latter, it was later established, had died just about this time.

Exercise C

Examine each of the following inductive arguments, having first indicated whether the conclusion is a generalization or a hypothesis. Even if the conclusion seems reasonable, look for such possible difficulties as faulty analysis of causal relations or the failure to take all factors into account.

1. "Macaulay [Johnson said], who writes the account of St. Kilda [an isolated island] . . . affirms for a truth, that when a ship arrives there, all the inhabitants are seized with a cold. Dr. John Campbell, the celebrated writer, took a great deal of pains to ascertain this fact, and attempted to account for it on physical principles, from the effect of effluvia from human bodies. . . . A Lady of Norfolk . . . has favored me with the following solution: 'Now for the explication of this seeming mystery. . . . Reading the book with my ingenious friend, the late Reverend Mr. Christian, of Docking—after ruminating a little, the cause, (says he,) is a natural one. The situation of St. Kilda renders a North-East Wind indispensably necessary before a stranger can land; the wind, not the stranger, causes an epidemic cold.' " (Boswell's *Life of Johnson*)

2. "The education, moral and intellectual, of every individual must be chiefly *his own work*. How else could it happen that young men, who have precisely the same opportunities, should be continually presenting us with such different results, and rushing to such opposite destinies? Difference of talent will not solve it, because that difference is very often in favor of the disappointed candidate.

You will see issuing from the walls of the same college—nay, sometimes from the bosom of the same family,—two young men, of whom the *one* shall be admitted to be a genius of high order, the *other* scarcely above the point of mediocrity; yet you shall see the genius sinking and perishing in poverty, obscurity, and wretchedness; while, on the other hand, you shall observe the mediocre plodding his slow but sure way up the hill of life . . . and mounting, at length, to eminence and distinction. . . ." (William Wirt)

3. "That men possess the productiveness which is called genius, and that women do not, is the one immutable distinction that is bound up with the intellectual idea of sex. We know that women have seldom, perhaps never, been great artists or great composers, and that the number of female writers who can be called great is very small as compared with those who make, or have made, literature the business of their life." (A. Orr)

4. The National Merit Scholarship Corporation was proud that 82 per cent of the National Merit Scholars ranked in the top quarter of their classes even though some went to colleges with very high standards. A critic in *Harper's Magazine* suggested that since the 3465 scholars surveyed had been selected from a group of 959,683 candidates, the results were not very spectacular—that in fact the selection procedures might have been faulty.

5. "If America has not had any great writers, the reason is given in these facts; there can be no literary genius without freedom of opinion, and freedom of opinion does not exist in America." (Alexis de Tocqueville in 1835)

6. It is not true that the number of Federal employees is excessive. There are only 1.3 Federal employees per hundred Americans today, compared to 1.6 in 1952. And of the 2,500,000 Federal civilian employees, 1,000,000 are employed by the Defense Department, 600,000 by the Post Office, 200,000 by the Veterans' Administration, and only 650,000 by all other government activities combined.

7. Recently the Civil Aeronautics Board refused to approve a merger of airline E and airline A. No explanation was given. It may be significant that two major stockholders of airline E are enemies of the present administration.

8. Socialized power is as dismal a failure in France as elsewhere. Production is 650,000 KWH per employee as compared to 1,700,000 per employee in the United States. Rates are fifteen to eighteen times as high as in 1938, whereas rates in the United States are down 38 per cent. In 1961 the average French price per KWH was 2.08 cents; in the United States the average price charged by private utilities was 1.82 cents. French rates are also higher than those of any other Common Market country. (After *Barron's Weekly*)

9. Offshore blasting in oil exploration doesn't hurt fishing. Blasting started this year, and this has been the best year for salmon in a long time.

10. If modern women seem less submissive, it is because men are less forceful.

11. "Television 'makes' delinquents of only those sad children who already showed severe signs of anti-social behavior, and who would probably have turned out to be delinquents anyway, given wretched homes and disgraceful parents." (*TV Guide*)

12. We should never allow ourselves to be lulled into the belief that Communism is not an immediate menace. One prominent Communist says that America is more ripe for revolution now than Russia was in 1917.

13. Can we doubt the immortality of the soul? A woman dreamed that her dead husband appeared to her and told her that her fears of death were groundless.

14. Certainly we could explain the flying saucers as the work of Martians; but we might just as well explain them as the work of ghosts, witches, or pagan gods.

15. "The ancients were convinced that dreams were usually supernatural. If the dream was verified, this was plainly a prophecy. If the event was the exact opposite of what the dream foreshadowed, the latter was still supernatural, for it was a recognised principle that dreams should sometimes be interpreted by contraries. If the dream bore no relation to subsequent events unless it were transformed into a fantastic allegory, it was still supernatural, for allegory was one of the most ordinary forms of revelation. If no ingenuity of interpretation could find a prophetic meaning in a dream, its supernatural character was even then not necessarily destroyed, for Homer said there was a special portal through which deceptive visions passed into the mind." (William Lecky)

16. "She was confident that burglars had been getting into her house every night for forty years. The fact that she never missed anything was to her no proof to the contrary. She always claimed that she scared them off before they could take anything, by throwing shoes down the hallway." (James Thurber)

17. "It was a good answer that was made by the man who was shown hanging in a temple a picture of those who had paid their vows as having escaped shipwreck. They would have

him say whether he did not now acknowledge the power of the gods. —'Aye,' asked he again, 'but where are they painted that were drowned after their vows?' " (Francis Bacon)

18. Love is all-important for young children. Formerly, in many orphanages, babies invariably died before the age of two. In a comparison of two institutions, in one of which the children were cared for by their mothers, and in the other by overworked nurses, it was found that children cared for by their mothers showed much better development.

19. ". . . There is much evidence to prove [the Irish fairies] fallen angels. Witness the nature of the creatures, their caprice, their way of being good to the good and evil to the evil, having every charm but conscience—consistency. . . . On the whole, the popular belief tells most about them, telling us how they fell, and yet were not lost, because their evil was wholly without malice." (W. B. Yeats)

20. "When [small gamblers] lose more than they can afford, they may become a nuisance to the community. According to the FBI's annual tally, Reno leads the nation in per-capita crime during most years. Its suicide rate is double the U.S. average. It has more murders than some cities four times as large." (*Harper's Magazine*)

V

LOGIC: *Deduction*

Deduction has already been defined as that form of reasoning wherein we put ideas together to see what can be inferred from them without further investigation; we reason, in other words, from premises to conclusions, not from facts to generalizations. The premises may themselves be the product of induction, and hence rooted in fact, but investigation of fact is not part of the deductive process itself. Consider the following arguments:

It is morally and economically wrong for either unions as unions or corporations as corporations to get into politics directly or indirectly. To me, it is wrong for the simple reason that it is wrong for any American to transfer his personal rights of citizenship to an institution. (George Romney)

What can be closer to the public interest than the health of women and their protection from unscrupulous and overreaching employers? And if the protection of women is a legitimate end of the exercise of State power, how can it be said that the requirement of the payment of a minimum wage fairly fixed in order to meet the very necessities of existence is not an admissable means to an end? (U.S. Supreme Court)

In arguments such as these, the writer tries to establish the truth of a proposition, not by offering factual evidence but rather by showing that it naturally follows from some other proposition whose truth has supposedly been established already. Mr. Romney tries to show that unions and corporations should not enter politics by reference to a broader rule that individuals should not give up political rights to institutions, while the Court's contention that a minimum wage for women is legitimate is based upon the assumption that the protection of the health of women is a proper function of the state. To be convinced by a deductive argument, we must, of course, be satisfied that the premises are sound; if we are not willing to grant that the protection of women's health is a proper function of the state, we may not be willing to go on to accept the idea of minimum wage. Furthermore, even if we accept the premises, we must be satisfied that the conclusion has been properly derived from them—that the reasoning is, in technical terms, *valid*.

What makes a deductive argument valid is its conformity to the rules of deductive reasoning. If these rules are followed, and if the premises are true, then the conclusion also must be true. If it is certain that all birds lay eggs, and certain that robins are birds, then it is not merely probable but necessarily true that robins lay eggs, since the line of reasoning is a valid one, conforming to the rules of the *syllogism*. If we are told that all trilobites are arthropods and that all arthropods are invertebrates, we can see that, according to the rules of sound deduction, all trilobites must be invertebrates, even though we do not happen to know what trilobites and arthropods may be.

The conclusions reached by deduction are regarded, therefore, as being not merely probable, like the conclusions of inductive reasoning, but as certainly and necessarily true, provided only that the premises are true and that the rules have been followed. This necessary character of deductive conclusions does not ensure that all valid deductive arguments lead to truth, for such arguments may be based on false premises. The following argument is valid, since the process of reasoning is perfectly correct, but the second premise being unhappily false, the conclusion remains unproved.

> If wishes were horses, beggars would ride.
> Wishes are horses.
> Therefore, beggars will ride.

Propositions

The premises and conclusions of deductive logic are propositions, that is, statements which can be affirmed or denied, which (unlike questions and commands) can be said to be true or false. Propositions may be divided into four classes:

1. *Universal affirmative propositions.* "All professors are wise," "All blondes are intelligent," "The Phoenix lives in Arabia." Such propositions assert that *all* members of a certain class have a certain characteristic. (It is perfectly possible for the class to consist of but one member, as in the case of the Phoenix.)
2. *Universal negative propositions.* "No men are infallible," "No women are good drivers." Such propositions state that all members of a certain class *lack* a certain characteristic.
3. *Particular affirmative propositions.* "Some students smoke," "Some mammals can fly." Such propositions assert that *some* members of the class have a certain characteristic.
4. *Particular negative propositions.* "Some women are

not married," "Some books don't have covers." Such propositions assert that *some* members of a class lack a certain characteristic.

The failure to distinguish among the various types may cause disorders in certain types of reasoning.

Immediate Inference

In general, as has been indicated already, deductive reasoning involves putting two propositions together to reach a conclusion different from either. In some cases, however, it is possible to reason from single propositions by a process known as *immediate inference*, which often involves simply reversing subject and predicate. Thus from the statement "No men are quadrupeds" it naturally follows that "No quadrupeds are men"; we know from the first statement that there is no being which is both a quadruped and a man, and so one universal negative implies the other. "No *X* are *Y*" always implies that "No *Y* are *X*." On the other hand, from "All *X* are *Y*" we can only infer that "*Some Y* are *X*"; for all we know from the first statement, *Y* may represent a large group that includes both *X*'s and non-*X*'s. Thus all wolves are mammals, but not all mammals are wolves; some are wolves, and some are elephants or animals of a thousand other different species. Curious as it seems, it is rather common to assume that "All *X* are *Y*" implies that "All *Y* are *X*." Thus it has been falsely argued that since geniuses tend to be odd, odd people are likely to be geniuses. In fact, it is just such simple inferences as this, which we make in an instant, scarcely conscious that we are reasoning, that are most likely to cause trouble.

Disjunctive Arguments

A *disjunctive* argument involves choosing between two alternatives. For instance:

> Lung cancer must be caused by smog or smoking.
> Smog has been proved not to be the cause.
> Therefore, smoking must be the cause.

The disjunctive argument starts with the assumption that one or the other of the possibilities must be correct and proceeds by elimination. There are two basic types, the *inclusive* and the *exclusive*. In the inclusive argument, it is assumed that one or both of the alternatives may be true; thus, in the argument above, it is perfectly possible that both smog and smoking might cause cancer. In such an argument, if one possibility is proved false, the other must be true; but if one is proved true, the other may still be true, or it may be false—only investigation can tell. Thus the following argument is obviously invalid:

> His poverty must be due to laziness or bad luck.
> He has had bad luck.
> Therefore, he isn't lazy.

There is nothing to prevent a man from being both lazy and unlucky. In the *exclusive* argument, it is assumed from the beginning that only one alternative is possible, and if we discover one to be true, we know the other to be false.

> She is either twenty or twenty-one.
> She is twenty-one.
> Therefore, she isn't twenty.

If there is any possible ambiguity, the first premise should be so stated as to show clearly whether the alternatives exclude each other or not. In some documents the inelegant phrase *and/or* is used to indicate inclusive alternation.

The chief difficulty in disjunctive arguments derives from using faulty premises—starting with alternatives that do not really exhaust the possibilities:

> His worn appearance must be due either to hunger or overwork. (But sickness is also possible.)
>
> A student who writes like this must be lazy or stupid or both. (But he might be ill-trained or distracted.)

One must be especially wary of the exclusive disjunctive argument, for all too frequently writers provide us with an either/or choice when in fact many alternatives are available to us. A further difficulty with exclusive arguments arises when the two alternatives are not really mutually exclusive; we may have only two choices open to us, but the nature of the alternatives does not prevent us from compromising between them.

> I must choose between a liberal education and learning to earn a living.
>
> I must learn to earn a living.
>
> Therefore, I can't have a liberal education.

> We must choose between the New Deal and the American Way of Life.
>
> We cannot give up the American Way of Life.
>
> Therefore, we must give up the New Deal.

In actuality most colleges offer various compromises between liberal and professional education, so that a student who has prepared himself to earn a living need not be an illiterate technician; and millions of Americans found at least the less radical proposals of the New Deal compatible with their way of life. The exclusive argument is common in political controversy and hence is to be treated with great caution.

Conditional Arguments

A *conditional* argument starts with the premise that, if certain circumstances are fulfilled, certain consequences will automatically follow. The following is a valid conditional argument:

> If he has fulfilled all requirements, he can graduate.
> He has fulfilled all requirements.
> Therefore, he can graduate.

All this is obvious enough, but it is not the only kind of valid inference which can be made from the premises. If, for instance, we find that the expected consequences have not followed, we can validly infer that the conditions have not been fulfilled.

> If this student were physically able, he would attend my interesting lecture.
> He is not attending my interesting lecture.
> Therefore, he is not physically able.

Or:

> If wishes were horses, beggars would ride.
> Beggars don't ride.
> Therefore, wishes aren't horses.

It is usually not legitimate, however, to reason that since the expected consequence has followed, the conditions must have been fulfilled. Consider the following argument:

> If this student were bored by my lecture, he would go to sleep.
> He is asleep.
> Therefore, he is bored by my lecture.

He might, after all, have fallen asleep because of exhaustion due to overwork or hell week. We might suggest boredom as a possible hypothesis (see Chapter IV), but since most events have more than one possible cause, we could not offer it as the necessary conclusion in a deductive argument.

Syllogism

The *syllogism* is at once a more common and a more complex form of argument than the disjunctive or the conditional argument. Like them, it simply makes explicit rather ordinary thought processes; like them, it leads from two premises to a conclusion, but differs in that the second premise does not qualify or modify the first premise but introduces an entirely new and independent proposition. (The second premise in a syllogism can, in another syllogism, be used as a first premise; the premises in disjunctive and conditional arguments are not, however, interchangeable in this way.) Furthermore, the syllogism can only function if it has three different *terms,* a term being a matter of discussion which appears in the subject or predicate of a proposition. One of these terms, the *middle* term, appears once in each premise but disappears in the conclusion. What the syllogism does is to relate two things or states of affairs to a third thing in order to show their relationship to each other. The following is a typical syllogism:

> All mammals are vertebrates.
> All elephants are mammals.
> Therefore, all elephants are vertebrates.

"All mammals," "all elephants," and "vertebrates" are the three terms. Knowing the connection between elephants and mammals (the middle term) and between mammals and vertebrates, we can infer the connection between elephants and vertebrates without opening an elephant to see whether it has a backbone. The process is somewhat analogous to the rule in plane geometry which states that things equal to the same thing are equal to each other; but the relationship between the terms of the syllogism is seldom that of equality. Elephants are not *equal* to vertebrates; they form part of the group of vertebrates. Usually a syllogism may be thought of as the application of a general rule to a specific situation. The general rule that mammals are vertebrates is applied to the specific case of elephants, and the elephants are found to be covered by the rule. Not all syllogisms follow this pattern exactly, but most approach it, and the application of general rule to particular case is one of the most important functions of the syllogism. (In a sense, we employ the syllogism every time we apply rule to case, though we do not ordinarily arrange our thoughts in syllogistic form.) It may also be helpful to think of the syllogism as defining the relationships among various classes of things. Since the class of vertebrates includes the class of mammals and the class of mammals includes the class of elephants, it is evident that the class of vertebrates must include the class of elephants. Similarly, the Supreme Court decision quoted at the beginning of this chapter argues that the minimum wage law falls within the class of acts protecting the health of women, which in turn belong to the class of acts promoting the public interest.

The syllogism has a number of variants which differ among themselves according to the arrangement of the terms in the premises and conclusion. The example of the elephant follows the simplest and most common pattern:

All *M* are *Y*.
All *X* are *M*.
Therefore, all *X* are *Y*.

(*M* will be used henceforth to stand for the middle term.)
The following syllogisms show the same pattern:

All passions are potentially dangerous.
Love is a passion.
Therefore, love is potentially dangerous.

All athletes are morally pure.
All tennis players are athletes.
Therefore, all tennis players are morally pure.

The next syllogism varies slightly from the foregoing in having one *particular* premise:

All interesting books are worth saving.
Some textbooks are interesting books.
Therefore, some textbooks are worth saving.

In this instance, only *some* (not all) textbooks are mentioned in the second premise, and so the conclusion can concern only *some* textbooks.

Very similar to this basic pattern is the following, which has the same types of premises but a different type of conclusion:

All mammals are vertebrates.
All elephants are mammals.
Therefore, some vertebrates are elephants.

(All *M* are *Y*.
All *X* are *M*.
Therefore, some *Y* are *X*.)

The conclusion is a *particular,* not a universal affirmative. Obviously it would be nonsense to conclude that *all* vertebrates are elephants; not only is this actually not the case, but it is a false conclusion from the premises, since we were not talking about *all* vertebrates in the first premise but only about those that are mammals. We can never enlarge the conclusion to cover something that is not in the premises. Another valid syllogism with a limited conclusion shows the following pattern:

> All mammals are vertebrates.
> All mammals are warm-blooded.
> Therefore, some vertebrates are warm-blooded.
>
> (All *M* are *X*.
> All *M* are *Y*.
> Therefore, some *X* are *Y*.)

Again, we cannot conclude that all vertebrates are warm-blooded (or that all warm-blooded animals are vertebrates, though that proposition happens to be true) since we were not talking about *all* vertebrates in the first place, but only about those which are mammals.

Unfortunately it is easy enough to make errors in relating the terms of the syllogism. A particularly unfortunate and particularly common pattern of error appears in the following invalid syllogism:

> All Fascists are opponents of labor unions.
> All reactionary Republicans are opponents of labor unions.
> Therefore, all Fascists are reactionary Republicans.
>
> (All *X* are *M*.
> All *Y* are *M*.
> Therefore, all *X* are *Y*.)

This kind of reasoning assumes that two things which have some characteristic in common or which belong to the same general class are identical in all respects, contrary to all logic and common sense. Fascists and reactionary Republicans might agree in opposing unions and disagree in everything else. It is easy to construct examples which expose the unsoundness of such an argument:

> All men are human beings.
> All women are human beings.
> Therefore, all men are women.

Clearly, men and women belong to the same general class, but they are not identical.

The premises in a syllogism need not be affirmative; one (but not both) may be negative. The valid conclusion may simply be that the rule expressed in the first premise does *not* apply to the case:

> All qualified voters are registered.
> X is not registered.
> Therefore, X is not a qualified voter.

> (All Y are M.
> X is *not* M.
> Therefore, X is not Y.)

Sometimes the main premise is itself negative, as in the following instances:

> No trees are animals.
> All oaks are trees.
> Therefore, no oaks are animals.

> (No M are Y.
> All X are M.
> Therefore, no X are Y.)

> No trees are animals.
> All trees are living things.
> Therefore, some living things are not animals.

(No *M* are *Y*.
All *M* are *X*.
Therefore, some *X* are not *Y*.)

It is not as easy to go wrong with negative arguments as with positive ones, but note the following:

All students are intelligent.
No professors are students.
Therefore, no professors are intelligent.

(All *M* are *Y*.
No *X* are *M*.
Therefore, no *X* are *Y*.)

The general class of the intelligent includes students but is not made up entirely of them; others fall within the class. The example given is obviously ridiculous, but the following chain of reasoning, though equally invalid, might be accepted by some:

All citizens are entitled to the protection of the laws.
No aliens are citizens.
Therefore, no aliens are entitled to the protection of the laws.

The first premise asserts that citizens belong to the class of those who are entitled to the protection of the laws, but it does not assert that others may not belong to this class; all *M* are *Y* does not imply that all *Y* are *M*.

The syllogism has 256 possible patterns, of which 24 produce valid conclusions. The patterns already cited have been given because they conform best to ordinary human thought processes; others tend either to represent the same processes in a slightly different form or to be so odd and complex that they are more suitable for puzzles than for essays. The following table sums up the patterns discussed and may be used for reference in criticizing arguments:

Valid: All *M* are *Y*.
          All (or some) *X* are *M*.
          Therefore, all (or some) *X* are *Y*.

          All *M* are *Y*.
          All *X* are *M*.
          Therefore, some *Y* are *X*.

          All *M* are *X*.
          All *M* are *Y*.
          Therefore, some *X* are *Y* (and some *Y* are *X*).

          All *Y* are *M*.
          No *X* are *M*.
          Therefore, no *X* are *Y*.

          No *M* are *Y*.
          All *X* are *M*.
          Therefore, no *X* are *Y*.

          No *M* are *Y*.
          All *M* are *X*.
          Therefore, some *X* are not *Y*.

Invalid: All *X* are *M*.
          All *Y* are *M*.
          Therefore, all *X* are *Y*.

          All *M* are *Y*.
          No *X* are *M*.
          Therefore, no *X* are *Y*.

In the examples given so far all the propositions have been in the form "All (some, no) *M* are *X*"—that is, they have all contained a form of the verb *to be*. Manifestly, assertions in actual arguments will not necessarily follow this form, nor is it absolutely necessary thus to frame the syllogism:

Whoever wrote *Hamlet* is a great writer.
Shakespeare wrote *Hamlet*.
Therefore, Shakespeare is a great writer.

There will be less likelihood of confusion and error, however, if all the propositions are cast in the "All are" form. So "Shakespeare wrote Hamlet" becomes "Shakespeare was the author of Hamlet"; a few further examples will illustrate the method of conversion:

"The state protects property" becomes "The state is the agency which protects property."

"Some mammals fly" becomes "Some mammals are creatures capable of flight."

Rules of the Syllogism

So far we have been content to exhibit arguments which show the commoner figures and to indicate in common-sense terms why they do or do not work. A logician would proceed somewhat differently; he would invoke the rules of the syllogism, which would be more reliable in excluding error than the rough-and-ready methods used above. What is given here is a slightly simplified version of these rules.

1. *The syllogism may have only three terms.* A valid argument with more than three terms would probably prove to be a *sorites* or series of syllogisms. Sometimes an unplanned fourth term creeps in because the middle term has shifted its meaning, thus:

All men are brothers.
All brothers are male siblings.
Therefore, all men are male siblings.

"Brothers" has shifted from its figurative to its literal meaning.

> No sane person drinks poison.
> Alcohol is a poison.
> Therefore, no sane person drinks alcohol.

Alcohol, though doubtless dangerous in certain quantities, is hardly a poison in the sense that arsenic is, so that "poison" cannot mean quite the same thing in the second premise that it did in the first.

2. *The syllogism cannot have two negative or two particular premises.* The consequences of either error can easily be seen:

> Some Americans are women.
> Some men are Americans.
> Therefore, some men are women.

> Some poor people are bad neighbors.
> Some clergymen are poor.
> Therefore, clergymen are bad neighbors.

> Some radicals are spies.
> Some professors are radicals.
> Therefore, some professors are spies.

To see the weakness of the latter argument, let us imagine a group of a thousand radicals of whom five are professors and five spies; the statistical probability that any of the professors are also spies is very small. From the fact that the class of professors and the class of spies overlap the class of radicals we cannot properly infer that the two classes overlap each other.

> No poor people are free men.
> No citizens of a welfare state are poor people.
> Therefore, citizens of a welfare state are free men.

The premises tell us that the class of poor people includes neither free men nor welfare state citizens, but they tell us nothing about the connection between the two latter classes. Perhaps some welfare state citizens are free, perhaps all, perhaps none, but if we wish to find out, we shall have to have a better starting-point than the premises given.

3. *If one premise is particular or negative, so is the conclusion.* We cannot go beyond the premises, as we would do if we jumped from *some X* or *no X* to *all X*.

4. *The middle term must be distributed at least once.* A *distributed* term is universal; it refers to all possible examples of the class. Obviously *subject* terms of universal propositions ("All men are mortal" or "No men are immortal") are universal; it is equally true but not so obvious that the predicate terms of negative propositions are likewise distributed. Thus in the propositions "No men are immortal" and "No aliens can vote" the terms "immortal" and "vote" are distributed in the sense that we absolutely exclude the possibility that an immortal being could be a man or a voter could be an alien; we really are saying something (however negative) about *all* immortals and *all* voters. This circumstance explains why the first syllogism given below is valid and the second invalid:

> No beasts are men.
> Adam is a man.
> Therefore, Adam is not a beast.

> Some men are lawyers.
> Some lawyers are women.
> Therefore, some men are women.

In the second case, "lawyers" is never distributed—we are never talking about *all* lawyers. For convenience, we may sum up the status of the various terms in tabular form:

Distributed Terms

Subject terms of all universal propositions.
Predicate terms of all negative propositions.

Undistributed Terms

Predicate terms of affirmative propositions.
Subject terms of all particular propositions.

5. *A term distributed in the conclusion must be distributed in the premise in which it appears.*   Again we cannot
jump from *some* to *all,* as in this example:

> Some students smoke.
> Those who smoke should be watched.
> Therefore, students should be watched.

"Students" has become distributed between the premise
and the conclusion. We started to talk about *some* students
and ended by talking about *all.*

It cannot be too much emphasized that these rules are
not the rules of an elaborate but useless game. Although
logic can be played as a kind of game or puzzle (as in
Lewis Carroll's *Symbolic Logic*), the rules themselves are
not arbitrary inventions but correspond to something in
the nature of reality and in the habits of human thought
at their best. They enable one to place one's own thinking
on a firmer foundation and to criticize the thinking of
others.

To illustrate the operations of syllogistic reasoning from
a practical instance of interest to all students of language,
let us consider the case of James Joyce's celebrated novel
Ulysses. For some time after its appearance in Europe, its
importation into the United States was blocked by Customs
officials on the grounds of obscenity; at length the ban was

lifted by the decision of Justice Woolsey, who reasoned, in part, as follows:

... Where a book is claimed to be obscene, it must first be determined, whether the intent with which it was written was what is called, according to the usual phrase, pornographic—that is, written for the purpose of exploiting obscenity. ... If the conclusion is that the book is pornographic that is the end of the inquiry and forfeiture [confiscation and destruction] must follow. ... The meaning of the word "obscene" as legally defined by the Courts is: tending to stir the sex impulses or to lead to sexually impure and lustful thoughts. ... After I had made my decision in regard to the aspect of *Ulysses* now under consideration, I checked my impressions with two friends of mine. ... I was interested to find that both agreed with my opinion that reading *Ulysses* ... did not tend to excite sexual impulses or lustful thoughts. ... *Ulysses* may, therefore, be admitted into the United States.

Put in syllogistic form, the argument might appear as follows:

All obscene books are books which lead to impure and lustful thoughts.
Ulysses is not a book which leads to impure and lustful thoughts.
Therefore, *Ulysses* is not an obscene book.

(All Y are M.
X is not M.
Therefore, X is not Y.)

Books which are not obscene are books which may be admitted to the United States.
Ulysses is a book which is not obscene.
Therefore, *Ulysses* is a book which may be admitted to the United States.

(All *M* are *Y*.

X is *M*.

Therefore, *X* is *Y*.)

It is interesting to note the source of the premises involved
in these syllogisms. The definition of "obscene" as tending
to lead to lustful thoughts is taken over from previous
court decisions. The premise that *Ulysses* does not lead to
impure thoughts, however, is a rough-and-ready inductive
generalization, obtained by testing whether the book in
fact aroused lustful feelings in Justice Woolsey and his
friends.

Such a combination of inductive and deductive reasoning is rather typical of human thinking. To take a docu-
ment more momentous than the *Ulysses* decision, we can
see the same combination in the Declaration of Independence. Here Jefferson and his colleagues had a double task.
Starting from the premise that "all men are created equal,"
they sought to prove deductively that a people had the
right to change its rulers under certain circumstances. But
they also had to prove that such circumstances existed in
1776, and this they did inductively by citing specific acts
of George III and Parliament which justified a change. In
any criminal trial, there is likely to be an inductive question: Did so-and-so commit such-and-such an act? And a
deductive question: Does such an act violate some particular law?

Problems of Deduction

There are certain difficulties in the handling of deductive logic. Not infrequently, as we have shown, the process
itself goes wrong and the conclusion does not constitute a
valid inference from the premises. Even though the process

itself is sound and the conclusion valid, however, there may still be trouble. From the point of view of the logician, the internal disorders of deduction—the errors in form, already discussed, which lead to invalid conclusions—are likely to be the center of attention, but the writer may have more trouble with the external difficulties that arise in applying deduction to practical situations.

We may, for instance, resort to deduction when a look at the concrete evidence would be more appropriate. We may do this out of indolence, or a theoretical habit of mind, or a fear that the evidence will not tell us what we want it to. Little Munro, in Jules Feiffer's story, is drafted at the age of four; he cannot get discharged because, as the sergeant puts it (without looking up from his desk), "It is not the policy of the Army to draft men of four; ergo, you cannot be four." It is a commonplace in Communist ideological thinking to infer what should logically follow from Marxian theory instead of seeing what the situation actually is. Anglo-Saxon political thinkers are supposed to be relatively free from such vices of thought, but one can find embarrassing exceptions. A professor at a western university was discharged on the reasoning that his adherence to a certain rather rigid political belief would inevitably lead him away from the unbiased pursuit of truth, in spite of unrefuted testimony which showed that he was in actuality a "sound" scholar and an "able and unbiased" teacher and that the subject he taught had no political significance. Lizzie Borden who "took an ax and gave her father forty whacks" was acquitted contrary to the weight of the evidence, apparently because the judge and jury could not bring themselves to believe that a respectable young woman would be capable of such a bloody crime. In this case the supposed premise, "No respectable young lady would kill her father with an ax," is probably at fault. A deductive argument, no matter how valid, is only as strong as its premises. Consider the following passage from G. K. Chesterton: "A Socialist Government is one which in its nature does not tolerate any true and real opposition. For there the Government provides everything; and it is absurd to ask a Government to *provide* an opposition." Such a train of reasoning can be forced into the form of a valid argument, but the effort is not worthwhile, since the premise "The Government provides everything" misrepresents Socialist thinking and describes an impossible situation. The following syllogism is formally valid:

> All people who cause pain to others are wicked.
> Surgeons are people who cause pain to others.
> Therefore, surgeons are wicked.

The first premise is rather inexactly expressed, however; if we wrote "All people who voluntarily and unjustifiably cause pain are wicked," the second premise could not be made and the absurd conclusion would disappear. In judging the premises, naturally, we go beyond the rules of deduction. If one or both premises are inductive generalizations, they must be judged in terms of the evidence that is used to support them; if they are basic principles, points of faith, or standards of value, then either they must be principles that the reader already accepts, or they must be supported by further argument or reference to some accepted authority, as when Justice Woolsey invoked an established rule of law. Sometimes a premise in a deductive argument is a definition, and then some caution is in order, as in the following instance:

Love has been defined by Plato, the Troubadours, and others as a longing for something that one does not possess; once satisfied, it must necessarily disappear. Hence it may be assumed that love will cease with marriage, since the longing will be satisfied.

The argument seems a strong one, but only as long as one does not challenge the definition of love; and since the definition does not follow ordinary usage, it is likely that many readers would reject the argument, holding that the state of satisfaction is likewise an example of love. In constructing deductive arguments, we must keep in mind that there is not much use in arguing from premises that the potential reader or hearer will not take for granted; the whole art of deduction in fact consists of advancing from premises already accepted to conclusions not yet accepted. An argument based on Papal Encyclicals will get one nowhere in a meeting of Quakers.

The task of criticizing deductive arguments would be much easier if premises were always clearly stated, but often at least one premise is omitted, either because a full statement would be clumsy and wordy or because the writer does not realize clearly what his premises are. This kind of condensed argument is so common that it has a technical name of its own, the *enthymeme*. Trouble arises when the writer reasons from an unstated assumption about which his reader (and perhaps he himself) would feel doubtful if it were stated in bald terms. The critic who said that "the best answer to the question why a jazz band should be spoken of as a serious musical enterprise is found in the box-office receipts" may really have believed that aesthetic matters could be judged in terms of money, or he may simply not have thought the matter through very clearly.

The professor who said that, since women have more genes than men, men are but imperfect women, could hardly have believed literally that value is determined by number of genes, but he seems to imply it. And does the political orator who argued that the Biblical commandment "Honor thy father and thy mother" obliges us to follow the monetary policies of the last generation really believe that we must follow the habits of our fathers in all respects? His argument is only valid on that assumption; one would like to know whether he owns a refrigerator, or whether he uses an icebox out of deference to his father.

Analogy

There is a peculiar and risky form of argument that can scarcely be classified as logical but which is so common as to demand discussion and can be most conveniently considered here since it involves a kind of unexpressed assumption. This is the *analogy*. In analogy we reason from parallel cases; that is, we assume that, since two things are known to be alike in certain respects, they will be alike in other respects. Since a national budget resembles a family budget in involving the allotment of a limited sum of money to meet certain necessary and some unnecessary expenses, some conservatives reason that in the national budget as in the family budget overspending will lead to disaster. (Liberals reason from the same analogy that national life requires planning just as family life does!) The unstated and unproved assumption is that all budgets are alike; it is unproved since it is based on the examination of only one instance, the household budget. In a sense, analogy telescopes the inductive and deductive processes. On the basis of an examination of one member of the class of budgets—the household budget—we conclude inductively that budgets must be made to balance, and using this conclusion as a premise, we reason deductively on national budgets:

> All budgets must be made to balance.
> A national budget is a budget.
> Therefore, a national budget must be made to balance.

It goes without saying that in a genuine inductive argument we should be very unlikely to generalize on so little evidence, and that in a genuine deductive argument we should be reluctant to reason from a premise supported by so little investigation.

Although all this would seem to imply that the analogy is the kind of argument that is better not employed at all, the device nevertheless has its uses. Often its function is more explanatory than argumentative; we reveal the nature of something remote or unknown by comparing it to something already clearly known:

. . . In our alertest moment the depths of the soul are still dreaming; the real world stands drawn in bare outline against a background of chaos and unrest. Our logical thoughts dominate experience only as the parallels and meridians make a checkerboard of the sea. They guide our voyage without controlling the waves, which toss for ever in spite of our ability to ride over them to our chosen ends. (George Santayana)

If, however, the analogy is meant to prove or to convince, it will be most plausible if the things compared are really closely related. Consider the following:

> A spaniel, a woman, and a walnut tree,
> The more they're beaten, the better they be.

The growth of a large business is merely a survival of the fittest. . . . The American Beauty rose can be produced in the splendor and fragrance which bring cheer to its beholder only by sacrificing the early buds which grow up around it. (J. D. Rockefeller)

The right which a people has to resist a bad government bears a close analogy to the right which an individual, in the absence of legal protection, has to slay an assailant. In both cases the evil must be grave. In both cases all regular and peaceable modes of defence must be exhausted before the agrieved party resorts to extremities. In both cases an awful responsibility is incurred. But in neither case can we absolutely deny the existence of the right. A man beset by assassins is not bound to let himself be tortured and butchered without using his weapons, because nobody has ever been able precisely to define the amount of danger which justifies homicide. Nor is a society bound to endure passively all that tyranny can inflict, because nobody has ever been able precisely to define the amount of misgovernment which justifies rebellion. (Thomas Babington Macaulay)

The first comparison is purely fanciful; the second brings together things really rather remote from each other, though showing one point of resemblance—the sacrificing of competitors; the third develops a whole series of parallels and succeeds in making its point. Before using even so plausible an analogy, one would naturally wish to consider whether some more satisfactory systems of proof might be available—preferably an inductive one. Such proof may not be always available, however, since we are not infrequently obliged to reason about situations, especially future situations, where inductive evidence is not forthcoming; in such a case, our duty would be not to avoid analogies but rather to select one which has the greatest possible relevance, the greatest number of points of real resemblance to the matter under discussion.

Final Remarks

We do not expect an ordinary essay or address to be cast in the rigorous forms of deductive logic. To get an argument into the form of a syllogism we should have to express it in the simplest possible terms, eliminating all emotional shades and rhetorical devices, very likely making it less rather than more convincing; whereas to produce a piece of effective communication, we might suppress obvious premises, invert premises and conclusions, recast propositions, and produce something perhaps not readily recognizable as a piece of syllogistic reasoning. But all this implies no real conflict between logic and rhetoric. Logic is the rule by which we measure the arguments of others, especially when common sense has already made us suspicious of them. It is likewise the rule by which we measure our own reasoning to see that it will have the effect we wish it to. If we think at all soundly, we will approximate the processes of logic; and it takes only a little effort to convert unconscious thinking or common sense to conscious reasoning. As the philosopher Croce puts it, "to reduce affirmations to a syllogistic form is a way of controlling one's own thought and of criticizing the thought of others. . . . Satire on it can concern only its abuses."

In examining deductive arguments in our *own* writing, then, we shall not be asking whether sentences mechanically fall into the patterns of the syllogism. Rather we shall question, first of all, the acceptability of premises: are they premises that the reader will take for granted, or will they require support from inductive or other proofs? Given the premises, we may then inquire whether the reasoning is valid—whether if reduced to syllogistic or other deductive patterns, it would stand the test of the rules. If we can answer both questions affirmatively, then at least the logic of the essay is sound, and what remains is a matter of art or rhetoric.

Exercises in Deduction

EXERCISE A

Reduce the following propositions to syllogistic form. Supply, in brackets, any implied premises. For example:

"Shakespeare cannot be a great writer, for he did not make up his own plots."

> [All great writers are writers who make up their own plots.]
> Shakespeare was not a writer who made up his own plots.
> Therefore, Shakespeare was not a great writer.

"The profit motive is bad, since all drive for power is bad."

> All drive for power is bad.
> [The profit motive is a drive for power.]
> Therefore, the profit motive is bad.

"It is undeniable that the exercise of a creative power, that a free creative activity, is the highest function of man; it is proved so by man's finding in it his true happiness." (Matthew Arnold)

> [That thing which produces true happiness is the highest function of man.]
> Exercise of creative power is that thing which produces true happiness.
> Therefore, exercise of creative power is the highest function of man.

1. Since he is a regular student, he must have passed the entrance examination.
2. If he's a wrestler, he can't have very high grades.

3. Since he isn't literate, he can't be an English major.

4. Since education is expected to prepare students for life, it must teach them to make decisions.

5. If the universe is fundamentally evil, we are better off not knowing the truth about it, for the truth would make us unhappy.

EXERCISE B

Examine the following passages and identify the type or types of argument employed. Formulate any assumptions or implied premises and comment on both the validity of the reasoning and the plausibility of the premises. (Do not confuse these two processes.) Many of the arguments are perfectly sound.

1. This student's paper seemed worth a "B" when I read it, but since he did badly on the aptitude test and had low grades in high school, I may have been wrong. I'll give him a "C."

2. If politicians can hire ghost writers, a student ought to be allowed to do the same thing.

3. An ROTC program is absolutely incompatible with the spirit of a university. A university strives to develop individuality, while the ROTC strives to regiment the individual.

4. "The argument, briefly put, is that because a social need exists the school must therefore attempt to satisfy it. This is a complete *non sequitur*. The school is only one of the agencies that exist to satisfy the needs of society. Each agency has its own area of responsibility, because each possesses a particular sort of competence. The particular competence of a school is in providing intellectual training." (Arthur Bestor)

5. "Given a crisis in any country in the world in which totalitarianism in any form threatens the liberty of its citizens, and the first to capitulate will be the non-religious educators. How could it be otherwise, for without a faith, how could they oppose a faith?" (Fulton J. Sheen)

6. "I talked of the recent expulsion of six students from the University of Oxford, who were Methodists and would not

desist from publicly praying and exhorting. JOHNSON. 'Sir, that expulsion was extremely just and proper. What have they to do at an University who are not willing to be taught, but will presume to teach? Where is religion to be learnt but at an University? Sir, they were examined, and found to be mighty ignorant fellows.' BOSWELL. 'But was it not hard, Sir, to expell them, for I am told they were good beings?' JOHNSON. 'I believe they might be good beings; but they are not fit to be in the University of Oxford. A cow is a very good animal in the field; but we turn her out of a garden.' Lord Elibank used to repeat this as in illustration uncommonly happy." (Boswell's *Life of Johnson*)

7. "The superiority of high art over the common or mechanical consists in combining truth of imitation with beauty and grandeur of subject. The historical painter is superior to the flower-painter, because he combines or ought to combine human interests and passions with the same power of imitating external nature. . . . The same argument might be applied to shew that the poet and painter of imagination are superior to the mere philosopher and man of science, because they exercise the powers of reason and intellect combined with nature and passion [while the scientist uses only reason]." (William Hazlitt)

8. "The exercise of the art of medicine ought, Plato said, to be tolerated, so far as that art may serve to cure the occasional distempers of men whose constitutions are good. As to those who have bad constitutions, let them die; and the sooner the better. Such men are unfit for war, for magistracy, for the management of their domestic affairs, for severe study and speculation. If they engage in any vigorous mental exercise, they are troubled with giddiness and fulness of the head, all which they lay to the account of philosophy. The best thing that can happen to such wretches is to have done with life at once."

9. "Exactly as the measure of our regard for the soldier who does his full duty in battle is the measure of our scorn for the coward who flees, so the measure of our respect for the true wife and mother is the measure of our scorn and con-

temptuous abhorrence for the wife who refuses to be a mother." (Theodore Roosevelt)

10. Why should I support my children? What have they done for me?

11. We cannot rightly execute for murder a man whose sanity is suspect, for if we do, we admit that the insane must be treated in the same way as the sane, and then we would have no right to lock up the violently insane until they actually commit crimes.

12. "The Declaration of Independence says all men are entitled to life, liberty, and the pursuit of happiness. When the University of A———— was integrated, the entire people of the South were denied liberty and happiness. This is dictatorship." (A Letter to an Editor)

13. "Many politicians of our time are in the habit of laying it down as a self-evident proposition, that no people ought to be free till they are fit to use their freedom. The maxim is worthy of the fool in the old story, who resolved not to go into the water till he had learned to swim! If men are to wait for liberty till they become wise and good in slavery they may, indeed, wait forever!" (Thomas Babington Macaulay)

14. Just as alloys make the toughest and most useful metals, so mixed races such as ours are the best.

15. Our problem is not economic; it is not political; it is ethical and moral.

16. Blaming a company for making big profits is like blaming a cow for giving too much milk.

17. "The notion that the colonel need be a better man than the private is as confused as the notion that the keӱstone need be stronger than the coping stone." (George Bernard Shaw)

18. "Is the League anti-capitalist? Of course it is. How otherwise could it stop war? How could we be against fascism without being against capitalism, seeing that fascism is an organized expression of capitalism in its declining period?" (Third Congress against War and Fascism, 1936)

19. "Which shall it be? Competitive enterprise with free-

dom of speech and the press, freedom of worship and assemblage, freedom to choose who shall rule over us; the state the servant of the people? Or, planned economy with the ultimate loss of every freedom our forefathers held dear; the people the servants of the state?" (Henning Webb Prentis, Jr.)

20. "You may say that for a socialist government to take away property from people is unjust and robbery; but is that really so? Suppose you found a number of children in a nursery all very dull and unhappy because one of them, who had been badly spoilt, had got all the toys together and claimed them all, and refused to let the others have any. Would you not dispossess the child, however honest its illusion that it was right to be greedy? That is practically the position of the property-owner today." (H. G. Wells)

21. "At present the State protects men in the possession and enjoyment of their property, and defines what that property is. The justification for its so doing is that its action promotes the good of the people. If it can be clearly proved that the abolition of property would tend still more to promote the good of the people, the State will have the same justification for abolishing property that it now has for maintaining it." (Thomas Huxley)

22. "There are only two motives that make human beings work. One of them is the fear of punishment and the other is the hope of reward. Fear of punishment is what drives the slave to toil under the lash of a superior or boss. The hope of profit or reward is the incentive that inspires the efforts of freemen. If you destroy the incentive system, what they call the capitalistic system, the profit system, you destroy the initiative of the American people. Instead of freemen toiling under the glorious inspiration of the hope of reward, we all become the slaves of the state, driven to our tasks by fear of punishment." (*Congressional Record*)

23. "However painful it is to us, we have to call a spade a spade in this letter. It seems to us that your novel is profoundly unjust, historically prejudiced in the description of the Revolution, the Civil War, and the post-revolutionary

years, is profoundly antidemocratic and alien to any conception of the interests of the people. . . . As people whose standpoint is diametrically opposite yours, we, naturally, believe that the publication of your novel in the columns of the magazine *Novy Mir* is out of the question." (Editors of the Soviet magazine *Novy Mir,* rejecting Pasternak's *Doctor Zhivago*)

24. "A government ought to contain in itself every power requisite to the full accomplishment of the objects committed to its care, and to the complete execution of the trusts for which it is responsible. . . . As the duties of superintending the national defence and of securing the public peace against foreign or domestic violence involve a provision for casualties and dangers to which no possible limits can be assigned, the power of making that provision ought to know no other bounds than the exigencies of the community. As revenue is the essential engine by which the means of answering the national exigencies must be procured, the power of procuring that article to its full extent must necessarily be comprehended in that of providing for those exigencies." (*Federalist Papers*)

25. "Say that civilization is a tree which, as it grows, continually produces rot and dead wood. The radical says: 'Cut it down.' The conservative says: 'Don't touch it.' The liberal compromises: 'Let's prune, so that we lose neither the old trunk nor the new branches.' " (Franklin D. Roosevelt)

26. "Survey the whole world, you will find that theft, murder, adultery, calumny, are regarded as offenses which society condemns and curbs; but should something approved in England and condemned in Italy be punished as if it were an outrage against all mankind? This is what I call a local offense. Doesn't something that is criminal only within the precincts of a few mountains or between two rivers require more indulgence of the judges than the outrages which are abhorred in all countries?" (Voltaire)

27. "No man can serve two masters: for either he will hate the one, and love the other; or else he will hold to the one,

and despise the other. Ye cannot serve God and mammon."
(New Testament)

28. "Or what man is there of you, whom if his son ask
bread, will he give him a stone? Or if he ask a fish, will he
give him a serpent? If ye then, being evil, know how to give
good gifts unto your children, how much more shall your
Father which is in heaven give good things to them that ask
him?" (New Testament)

Exercise C

1. Select an argumentative passage from a newspaper or a
   popular magazine and reduce it to syllogistic form. A passage of whose validity you have doubts would be especially
   interesting.
2. Provide an outline in syllogistic form for one of your own
   themes.

CONCLUSION

CONCLUSION

The treatment of semantics and logic in this volume has necessarily been brief. If the brevity is sometimes tantalizing, this may be all to the good; such an introduction will be especially valuable if it stimulates an appetite for further work among the standard offerings of a philosophy department. Even an elementary treatment, however, may be of immense use in solving the practical problems of reading and writing. Many specific practical applications have been suggested in the course of the text. We might sum them all up by saying that these disciplines increase our conscious control over the language we use and increase our sense of responsibility in using it. Ever since the ancient Greeks discovered that methods of persuasion could be analyzed and taught, it has been understood that language is a potent weapon for good or evil, and in the eyes of some thinkers both ancient and modern, language and its arts have been regarded with no little suspicion. To such suspicions there is no better answer than Aristotle's:

If it is argued that one who makes an unfair use of such faculty of speech may do a great deal of harm, this objection applies equally to all good things except virtue, and above all to those things which are most useful, such as strength, health, wealth, generalship; for as these, rightly used, may be of the greatest benefit, so wrongly used, they may do an equal amount of harm.

The effect of language in molding human life has doubtless been exaggerated, but no one would deny that it is enormous, and that the careless or unscrupulous use of language does incalculable harm. If logic and semantics can decrease the damage even a little, we are that much nearer to the reign of reason in human affairs.

Review Exercise

Examine the following passages in the light of all the problems discussed in the course of the book. *Look not only for fallacies and deceptive uses of language, but also for effective arguments and skillful uses of language.*

1. "There ain't no sin and there ain't no virtue. There's just stuff people do. It's all part of the same thing. And some of the things folks do is nice, and some ain't nice, but that's as far as any man got a right to say." (*The Grapes of Wrath*)

2. Teachers have no right to think as they please unless they please to think right.

3. "Those who would legislate against the teaching of evolution should also legislate against gravity, electricity, and the unreasonable velocity of light." (Luther Burbank)

4. Scientists claim to be objective, but they must use numbers, which only exist in the mind, and since everything in the mind is by definition subjective, scientists are subjective too.

5. "A rock is nothing else than a society of molecules, indulging in every species of activity open to molecules. I draw attention to this lowly form of society in order to dispel the notion that social life is a peculiarity of the higher organisms. The contrary is the case." (Alfred North Whitehead)

6. "I asked him whether, as a moralist, he did not think

that the practice of the law, in some degree, hurt the nice feeling of honesty. JOHNSON. 'Why no, Sir, if you act properly. You are not to deceive your clients with false representations of your opinion: you are not to tell lies to a judge.' BOSWELL. 'But what do you think of supporting a cause which you know to be bad? JOHNSON. "Sir, you do not know it to be good or bad till the Judge determines it. I have said that you are to state facts fairly; so that your thinking, or what you call knowing, a cause to be bad, must be from reasoning, must be from supposing your arguments to be weak and inconclusive. But, Sir, that is not enough. An argument which does not convince yourself, may convince the Judge to whom you argue it; and if it does convince him, why, then, Sir, you are wrong and he is right. It is his business to judge. . . .' " (Boswell's *Life of Johnson*)

7. ". . . In 1787 one of the declared objects for ordaining and establishing the Constitution was 'to form a more perfect union.' But if the destruction of the Union by one or by a party only of the States be lawfully possible, the Union is less perfect than before the Constitution, having lost the vital element of perpetuity. It follows . . . that no State of its own mere motion can lawfully get out of the Union." (Abraham Lincoln)

8. ". . . I respect the conservative temper. I claim to be an animated conservative myself, because being a conservative I understand to mean being a man who not only preserves what is best in the Nation but who sees that in order to preserve it you dare not stand still but must move forward. The virtue of America is not statistical; it is dynamic." (Woodrow Wilson)

9. A democratic government cannot be said to own property, for the government can always be changed by the voters, and then it will no longer own the property.

10. "The machinery of communism like existing human machinery, has to be framed out of existing human nature and the defects of existing nature will generate in the one the same evils as in the other. . . . There is no political alchemy

by which you can get golden conduct out of leaden instincts."
(Herbert Spencer)

11. "These so-called right-to-work laws grant no one an actual right to work. They create not a single new job. A worker
receives merely the 'right not to join a union' in a plant where
the majority of the workers want a union. This has all the attraction and value of the 'right not to eat' and the 'right not
to get a living wage.' " (George Meany)

12. "Liberty is to faction what air is to fire, an aliment
without which it instantly expires. But it could not be less
folly to abolish liberty, which is essential to political life, because it nourishes faction, than it would be to wish the an-
nihilation of air, which is essential to animal life, because it
imparts to fire its destructive agency." (*Federalist Papers*)

13. ". . . Having paid a first-class fare for the entire journey
from Chicago to Hot Springs, and having offered to pay the
proper charge for a seat which was available in the Pullman
car for the trip from Memphis to Hot Springs, he was com-
pelled, in accordance with custom, to leave that car and ride
in a second-class car and was thus denied the standard convenience and privileges afforded to first-class passengers. This
was manifestly a discrimination against him in the course of
his interstate journey and admittedly that discrimination was
based solely upon the fact that he was a Negro. . . . The de-
nial to appellant of equality of accommodations because of his
race would be an invasion of a fundamental individual right
which is guaranteed against state action by the Fourteenth
Amendment. . . ." (U.S. Supreme Court)

14. ". . . It may be said that if, in the interest of the public welfare, the police power may be invoked to justify the
fixing of a minimum wage, it may, when the public welfare is
thought to require it, be invoked to justify a maximum wage.
. . . If, for example, in the opinion of future lawmakers,
wages in the building trades shall become so high as to pre-
clude people of ordinary means from building and owning
homes, an authority which sustains the minimum wage will
be invoked to support a maximum wage for building laborer

and artisans, and the same argument which has been here urged to strip the employer of his constitutional liberty of contract in one direction will be utilized to strip the employee of his constitutional liberty of contract in the opposite direction." (U.S. Supreme Court)

15. How can you call this man a Communist just because he writes regularly for Communist magazines? Are all the people who write for women's magazines women?

16. "Rum is vile and deadly and accursed everywhere. The poet would liken it in its fiery glow to the flames that flicker around the abode of the damned. The theologian would point you to the drunkard's doom, while the historian would unfold the dark record of the past and point you to the fate of empires and kingdoms lured to ruin by the siren song of the tempter, and sleeping now in cold obscurity, the wrecks of what once were great, grand and glorious. Yes, rum is corrupt and vile and deadly, and accursed everywhere. Fit type and semblance of all earthly corruption!" (*The Complete Speaker and Reciter*)

17. "We have forgotten that a society progresses only to the extent that it produces leaders that are capable of guiding and inspiring progress. And we cannot develop such leaders unless our standards of education are geared to excellence instead of mediocrity. We must give full rein to individual talents, and we must encourage our schools to enforce the academic disciplines—to put preponderant emphasis on English, mathematics, history, literature, foreign languages and the natural sciences." (Barry Goldwater)

18. "Many of the developing nations are wanting in private capital which is the very basis of free enterprise. But in the long run, the conviction grows that growth, freedom, and prosperity can be achieved only through the acceptance and practice of free enterprise—attracting outside capital—encouraging the formation of private capital—offering profit incentives. At least in those countries where I visited there was a notable difference in the condition of the economy and the drive of the people where this was being done.

"The profit motive in free, competitive climates motivates the creativity, innovation, and efficiency so desperately needed to accelerate the development of skilled technicians and managers, of agricultural and natural resources. Thus the growing nations are benefiting from free competitive enterprise and the profit incentive." (William T. Brady)

19. The miracles supposed to have been performed at the tomb of the Abbé Paris were investigated on the spot by judges of unquestioned integrity and attested by creditable witnesses. Hostile critics were completely unable to detect any imposture. Nevertheless, such miracles could not have taken place, because they are impossible. (After Hume)

20. "The country's doubts about the loyalty of its citizens are not unlike the doubts of a husband about the fidelity of his wife. The protestations that answer his doubts are never convincing and are likely to dissipate the mutual confidence that is the essence of a marriage. When men lose faith in one another, they lose the substance of what constitutes a community among them. Thus, to a national community, there is nothing that so dangerously corrupts its integrity as such a loss of faith. As in the case of the suspicious husband, this distrust is the expression of a neurotic insecurity." (Alan Barth)

21. "It is said that 'comic books must be all right because they are so widespread.' (That is like saying that infantile paralysis is all right because so many children have it.)" (Dr. Frederic Wertham)

22. "The idea that marriage must be coextensive with love or even affection nullifies it altogether. . . . We should have to reword the marriage vow. Instead of saying, 'till death do us part,' we might say, 'till we get bored with each other'; and, instead of 'forsaking all others,' 'till someone better comes along.' Clearly, if the couple intend to stay 'married' only as long as they want to, they only pretend to be married: they are having an affair with legal trimmings. To marry is to vow fidelity regardless of any future feeling. . . ." (Ernest van den Haag)

23. "Now what's the *use* of prying into the philosophical basis of morality? We all know what morality is: it is behaving as you were brought up to behave; that is, to think you ought to be punished for not behaving. But to believe in thinking as you have been brought up to think defines *conservatism*. It needs no reasoning to perceive that morality is conservatism. But conservatism again means, as you will surely agree, not trusting to one's reasoning powers. To be a moral man is to obey the traditional maxims of your community without hesitation or discussion. Hence ethics, which is the reasoning out of an explanation of morality, is—I will not say immoral, that would be going too far—composed of the very substance of immorality." (C. S. Peirce)

24. "Either we have an immortal soul, or we have not. If we have not, we are beasts; the first and wisest of beasts, it may be; but still true beasts. We shall only differ in degree, and not in kind; just as the elephant differs from the slug. But by the concession of all the materialists of all the schools, or almost all, we are not of the same kind as the beasts—and this also we say from our own consciousness. Therefore, methinks, it must be the possession of a soul within us that makes the difference." (Samuel Taylor Coleridge)

25. "Was all to die with our bodies, there might be some pretence for those different sorts of happiness, that are now so much talked of; but since our all begins at the death of our bodies; since all men are to be immortal, whether in misery or happiness, in a world entirely different from this; since they are all hastening hence at all uncertainties, as fast as death can cut them down; some at midnight, others at cock-crowing, and all at hours they know not of; is it not certain that no man can exceed another in joy and happiness, but so far as he exceeds him in those virtues which fit him for a happy death?" (William Law)

26. "I told him that a foreign friend of his . . . said to me, 'I hate mankind, for I think myself one of the best of them, and I know how bad I am.' JOHNSON. 'Sir, he must be very singular in his opinion, if he thinks himself one of the best

of men; for none of his friends think him so.' . . . I mentioned Hume's notion, that all who are happy are equally happy; a little miss with a new gown at a dancing school ball, a general at the head of a victorious army, and an orator, after having made an eloquent speech in a great assembly. JOHNSON. 'Sir, that all who are happy, are equally happy, is not true. A peasant and a philosopher may be equally *satisfied*, but not equally *happy*. Happiness consists in the multiplicity of agreeable consciousness. A peasant has not capacity for having equal happiness with a philosopher.' I remember this very same question very happily illustrated in opposition to Hume, by the Reverend Mr. Robert Brown, at Utrecht. 'A small drinking-glass and a large one, (said he,) may be equally full; but the large one holds more than the small.' " (Boswell's *Life of Johnson*)

APPENDIXES

The validity of syllogisms may be conveniently tested through the use of the Venn diagram, a set of three overlapping circles; each circle represents a term, and the type of overlapping indicates the relationships. The method will be clearer if we illustrate first with simple propositions of two terms. "All *M* are *X*" would be represented thus:

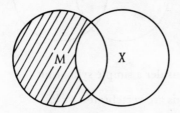

The part of circle *M* lying outside circle *X* has been shaded to symbolize that there is no member of class *M* which is not also a member of class *X*. No *M* are *X*, on the other hand, would be symbolized by shading the overlapping parts of the circles:

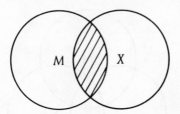

Some *M* are *X* would be symbolized by an asterisk in the overlap:

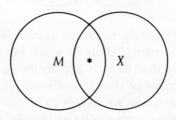

(No part of *M* is shaded, since we know that part of class *M* lies outside class *X*.) Some *M* are not *X* would be symbolized thus:

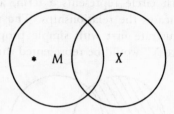

Now let us consider a simple syllogism:

> All mammals are vertebrates.
> All elephants are mammals.
> Therefore, all elephants are vertebrates.

One circle (*M*) will stand for mammals, one (*V*) for vertebrates, and one (*E*) for elephants:

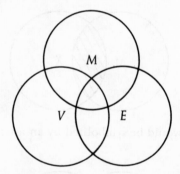

Since according to the premises all mammals are vertebrates, we will shade the part of circle *M* which lies outside circle *V*, thus symbolizing that there is no member of class *M* which is not also a member of class *V*, and since the premises tell us that there is no elephant which is not a mammal, we will shade all of circle *E* which does not lie within circle *M:*

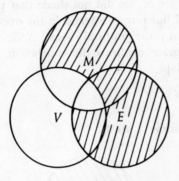

Since the only part of circle *E* which remains unshaded lies within circle *V*, the conclusion that all elephants are vertebrates is confirmed. Notice, too, that another possible valid conclusion from the premises—"Some vertebrates are elephants"—is confirmed by the fact that part of circle *V* lies within circle *E*. Likewise the conclusion "All vertebrates are elephants" is clearly shown to be invalid, since so much of circle *V* lies outside circle *E*.

Some other valid patterns will diagram as follows:

All *M* are *Y*.
Some *X* are *M*.
Therefore, some *X* are *Y*.

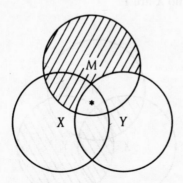

Since not all *X* are *M,* we did not shade that part of *X* which lay outside of *M* but put an asterisk in the overlapping section to symbolize that some (and only some) *X* lie within the class of *M.* The diagram confirms the conclusion, since circles *X* and *Y* still overlap.

> All *M* are *X.*
> All *M* are *Y.*
> Therefore, some *X* are *Y.*

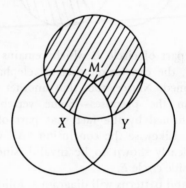

Since circles *X* and *Y* overlap, the conclusion is confirmed.

> All *Y* are *M.*
> No *X* are *M.*
> Therefore, no *X* are *Y.*

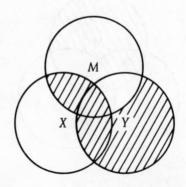

Since no X are M, we shaded the portion of the diagram where these circles overlap; and when we have also shaded that part of Y which lies outside M, we find that X and Y no longer overlap, and the conclusion is confirmed.

No M are Y.
All X are M.
Therefore, no X are Y.

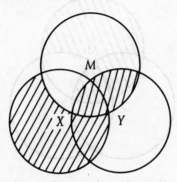

When we have shaded that part of X which lies outside M and that part of M which overlaps Y, we find that X and Y no longer overlap.

The diagrams will also serve to detect invalid reasoning:

All X are M.
All Y are M.
Therefore, all X are Y.

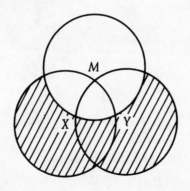

Since much of circle X still lies outside circle Y—symbolizing that it is possible to be X and not Y—the conclusion is shown to be invalid.

All M are Y.
No X are M.
Therefore, no X are Y.

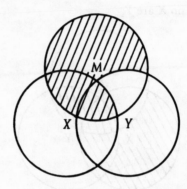

Since X and Y still overlap, the conclusion is shown to be invalid.

Appendix B: Fallacies

Logic texts often offer a list of common fallacies or errors in reasoning, usually an adaptation of a standard list which goes back to Aristotle. Fallacies may be classified as *material,* involving a mishandling of the facts; *verbal,* involving a misuse of words; and *formal,* involving errors in deductive reasoning.

I. MATERIAL FALLACIES

Some of these work by oversimplifying the issues. Such are:

Accident. A general rule is applied regardless of the special circumstances. "He's a murderer and ought to be hanged, no matter what you can say in his defense."

Black-and-white fallacy. It is argued that there are only two possibilities in a situation, and no other alternatives are possible. "It's either the American highway to freedom, or the Socialist hand-out highway to dictatorship."

Other fallacies work by distracting the reader's attention from the real issues. Such are:

Ad hominem. One attacks the personal character of an opponent instead of answering his arguments. "All this trouble is due to outside agitators." "The decision to allow the sale of *Lady Chatterley's Lover* must be wrong. The judge who ruled for the book was an associate of an opponent of Senator McCarthy, and a critic who testified was born in Brooklyn of Russian parents."

Ad populum. This is an appeal to popular opinion or prejudice. The "bandwagon" technique of urging the reader to do as everyone else does is a variant.

Among the material fallacies we would also put those which employ irrelevant evidence, as:

Appeals to tradition and authority. These are only fallacious if the authority is unqualified or the tradition unacceptable. See pp. 43–44, 58–59.

Apriorism. This is the use of deductive reasoning where inductive would be more appropriate. See pp. 99–100.

Here too belong the inductive errors discussed in Chapter IV.

Hasty generalization.
Post hoc ergo propter hoc.
Complex hypotheses.

II. VERBAL FALLACIES

The most important is *equivocation,* the use of a term in different senses in the same argument. See pp. 16–17.

III. FORMAL FALLACIES

These are violations of the rules of deductive reasoning.

Four terms. See pp. 93–94.

Undistributed middle. See pp. 95–96.

Illicit process. This occurs when a term undistributed in the premises is distributed in the conclusion. See p. 95.

Negative premises. See pp. 94–95.

Begging the question. In such an argument, one premise and the conclusion are virtually equivalent, so that a proposition is made to prove itself. "It must be a reliable company—its advertisements say so." (But we should believe the advertisements only if we already know the company to be reliable.)

Set in Linotype Baskerville
Composed by American Book–Stratford Press
Printed by The Murray Printing Company
Bound by The Murray Printing Company
HARPER & ROW, PUBLISHERS, INCORPORATED